Girls' Guide to POKER

Girls' Guide to POKER

Eliza Burnett

hamlyn

First published in Great Britain in 2007 by
Hamlyn, a division of Octopus Publishing Group Ltd
2–4 Heron Quays, London E14 4JP

Distributed in the United States and Canada by
Sterling Publishing Co., Inc.
387 Park Avenue South, New York, NY 10016-8810

ISBN-13: 978-0-600-61591-0
ISBN-10: 0-600-61591-X

A CIP catalogue record for this book
is available from the British Library

Printed and bound in United Arab Emirates

10 9 8 7 6 5 4 3 2 1

contents

Introduction

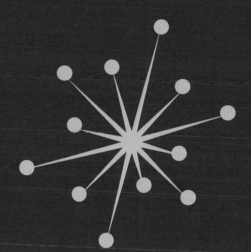

A short history
What every girl needs to know about poker

The origins of poker are a matter of hot debate. Some say that it is derived from the 16th-century Persian card game *As Nas*, but others claim that its roots lie in the French game of *Poque* or the German game of *Pochspiel*. The games of *Brag* and *Brelan* also influenced the development of modern poker.

Poker has shrugged off its image as a seedy game played in smoke-filled rooms frequented by gangsters and has developed into a respectable pastime for everyone. In recent years, the poker phenomenon has exploded, with literally millions of people playing at any time of the day or night, at home, in casinos or online around the world.

The extraordinary growth of the online game has boosted the current popularity of poker. Television, too, has played a huge part in its revival, bringing poker to millions of new fans. The audience has become part of the game: the players' cards are revealed to the screen audience and commentators explain the possible outcomes of the hands. Players have become overnight celebrities after winning televised events.

Prize money up for grabs in the big worldwide tournaments is huge and it keeps on growing. In 2000, Chris 'Jesus' Ferguson won the World Series of Poker Championship along with $1.5 million. In 2006, Jamie Gold won the coveted prize and his prize money amounted to $12 million. Staggering numbers of women are flocking to the game and succeeding – events exclusively for women are now held worldwide. Women have arrived on the scene to beat the men at their own game!

Poker is all about making the right decisions at the right time, guessing what your opponent may be holding and playing your cards accordingly. At the same time you try to make your opponents play their hands differently by masking the strength of your own hand.

This book aims to get you started by teaching you the basics of No Limit Texas Hold'em, described as the 'Cadillac' of poker games. It is very easy to pick up but will take a lifetime to master. And because it involves a degree of luck as well as skill, anyone can sit down at the table and join the party!

Poker appeal
Girl power!

Thanks to the growth of high-speed Internet access in so many homes, poker popularity has spread like wild-fire, and players around the globe have latched on to the intriguing world of online poker.

The natural progression from playing online is to venture out and play live in 'bricks and mortar' games. The old image of dark, smoky card rooms has long been dispelled as poker hits the 21st century. The game of choice over the last few years is No Limit Texas Hold'em. This much faster-paced variation with the added option of pushing your chips 'all-in' is pure heart-pounding excitement.

What is really exciting is that as women we naturally have the edge over men – unlike other sports where strength, speed, weight or other factors tend to tip the balance in favour of men, poker is tailor-made for women. Let's look at this more carefully. The key criteria in making a good poker player are listed below and let's face it, we women have them all in spades!

Flaunt your womanly assets

Patience is that asset and is also one of the key elements in the game. You will need a lot of it as most games last three or more hours and in that time you will see very few good hands, so waiting for the right time is paramount to your success. Have you ever met a man with any patience? We spend our lives waiting on them and don't often complain. We take a few extra minutes to get ready and they moan. Slow and steady is the order of the day.

I can read you like a book!

The ability to read your fellow players is vital to poker success. Are they holding a monster hand or are they weak? Determining this will establish your success. I don't know about you, but most men I know are the worst judges of character. Bring on that famous female intuition!

Give a star performance

Having the skill to bluff by making your opponent lay down a reasonable hand when you are not holding the best cards will gain you many chips in between your 'good' hands. Not many men can bluff without giving off signals, whereas we women can convince that black is white, when necessary. Use those acting skills!

These three key areas of poker make it a must for women not only to get involved but to reap rewards using our canny insight and advantages against male opponents. And don't discount the value of a pretty female face – the male to female ratio is 50:1 and if you, literally, play your cards right you could come home with a healthy profit and crush a few male egos along the way.

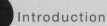
Playing live vs online poker
Facing real people or your PC

Whether you play live in a casino or in an online card room it is fundamentally the same game – No Limit Texas Hold'em. There are advantages and disadvantages to both and in time you will come to recognize what suits you.

Playing live in a casino or in a home game has lots of social advantages. Being around your friends or fellow enthusiasts certainly brings the game alive. The down-side is that games may well be limited depending on space or interest, and only some levels will be catered for unless you visit the big supercasinos in Las Vegas where the world is your oyster. Tournaments may not begin when it is convenient for you or you may live a long distance from your nearest casino.

There is more to think about when playing live – table etiquette and picking up 'tells' (nervous twitches or habits) on your fellow opponents for a start. There are less hands per hour due to shuffling and dealing of each hand and possible table charges. You might have to wait a while until a seat becomes available.

Online, however, the multitude of games available to you day and night is unlimited. Whether you choose to play a cash game ranging from micro-limits to high stakes, short handed or ring games,

the list is endless. For tournaments, the choice is like a superstore. Multi-table tournaments start with buy-ins from as little as a dollar and are sometimes free to enter (known as free rolls). Single table tournaments are great to play as they can complete quite quickly and give you practice for those final tables you are destined to reach!

Satellite tournaments are sometimes available. These are tournaments where you can enter a smaller tournament and win a seat into a larger one.

Play to suit your purse

Day or night, you can always find a game that suits your bankroll. Some people multi-table, which means they play more than one game at once on the same screen. This is not recommended for beginners since you need experience to juggle between the games and mistakes are easily made. You can also play for free money on most sites to get a feel for the game. These are helpful up to a point but if you are not playing for money you will find the decisions you make are very different.

Playing online can get a bit tedious and it is very easy to get distracted by the telephone or e-mails. It is also very easy to lose control of your bankroll as reloading your account via your credit card is all too easy after a losing streak. Discipline is paramount on the Internet (as well as playing live) and you should have some personal rules when playing to avoid big money swings.

Online you can pick up 'tells' on the other players by looking at their betting patterns, the time it takes them to act and the frequency of their play. Some sites offer a note-making facility where you can write down your observations.

And last but not least, online no one will know that you are a woman (unless you tell them!) and poker then becomes a game of complete equality.

Worldwide tournaments
Show me the money!

Tournament poker has exploded in the last decade and the biggest of them all is the World Series of Poker (WSOP). This takes place once a year in Las Vegas and attracts poker players from around the world. The winner of each tournament is presented with a coveted gold bracelet, the equivalent of winning a gold medal at the Olympics in poker terms.

Money-making marathon

The WSOP made its official debut in 1970 but the idea was actually conceived two decades earlier in 1949. The story goes that gambler Nicholas 'Nick the Greek' Dandolos approached casino owner Benny Binion with an unusual request – to challenge the best player in a high-stakes poker marathon. Binion agreed to set up the marathon between Dandolos and professional gambler, the legendary Johnny Moss, with the stipulation that the game must be played in public view. During the five-month-long marathon (with breaks only for sleep), the two men played every form of poker imaginable. Moss ultimately won 'the biggest game in town' and an estimated $2 million. It captured the public's imagination and led to what is now known as the WSOP.

Big stakes, big jackpots

Most forms of poker are played at the WSOP but the one everyone wants to win is the main event, usually a $10,000 entry. In 2006 this event attracted nearly 9,000 entrants with the winner Jamie Gold winning $12 million and a place in history. There are around 40 events during the series including a hotly contested ladies' event.

Touring around

For the rest of the year the focus spreads around the world. The World Poker Tour (WPT) makes its way around America and a couple of other countries and attracts some of the best players in the world. The Tour is televised across America on Wednesday evenings and attracts over 25 million viewers a season.

The European Poker Tour (EPT) was started in 2004 by John Duthie. These are large buy-in tournaments that tour around Europe and culminate in a Grand Final. The first woman to win an EPT event was Victoria Coren who won £500,000 in the London leg in 2006. The EPT is televised and has added a lot of glitz and glamour to poker along with the vast prize-pools that attract the big American players.

Poker afloat

Other big money tournaments are held year-round, some in exotic Caribbean locations or on board large cruise ships. One of the most popular is the Partypoker.com Million, which takes place in the spring on board a luxury liner and guarantees $1 million prize-pools.

Most big tournaments have a proportion of players who have qualified from next to nothing by playing small games on the Internet and climbing up the ladder via satellites.

The most famous online qualifier to date is Chris Moneymaker who won his seat to the WSOP main event for $39 and went on to become World Champion with a $2.5 million first prize.

Hand rankings
What beats what?

It is important to know the order or rankings of poker hands.
The following sequence applies in all variations of the game.

Royal flush

The most famous and the only unbeatable hand in poker is a royal flush – 10, J, Q, K, A.

Straight flush

The combination of a flush and a straight – your hand must contain five consecutive cards, all of the same suit. In the unlikely event of two straight flushes turning up, the highest-ranking straight flush prevails.

Four of a kind

A set of four cards, all of which are the same number.

Full house

A set of five cards that consists of a pair and three of a kind together. In the event of a tie, the value of the three cards dominates and thus a full house of 3, 3, 4, 4, 4 wins over a full house of 3, 3, 3 , 4, 4.

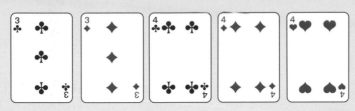

Flush

A flush is any hand where all five cards of any value are the same suit. If two players hold a flush the player holding the highest-ranking card is the winner.

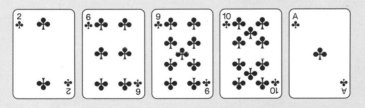

Straight

A straight is five cards with consecutive values such as 5, 6, 7, 8, 9. If two players have straights, the player holding the higher-ranked straight is declared the winner. In the event of a straight with A, 2, 3, 4, 5 against a straight with 3, 4, 5, 6, 7, the latter is the higher-ranked straight as the Ace in the first hand is being used as a low card. A straight of equal cards from two players results in a shared pot.

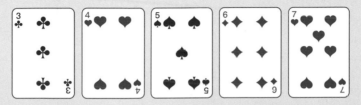

Three of a kind

This is when your hand has three cards of the same value.

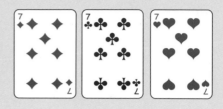

Two pairs

Self-explanatory – you have two pairs from the cards available. If two players each have two pairs, the player with the highest pair is the victor and the supplemental pair is ignored. If two players both hold the same top pair, then the secondary pair determines the victor. If the second pair is also identical then the last card in their hand of the five nominated cards will break the tie. If this is also equal then the pot is split.

One pair

Again, this hand is when you have a single pair from the cards available. If two players have a pair the higher-ranked pair wins the pot. If the pair the two players are holding is the same, then the next highest card in their hand is used to break the deadlock. This continues through all the remaining cards until one hand is superior. If both have the exact same hand then the pot is split.

High card

This occurs when neither of your two 'hole' cards (cards dealt face down and not revealed until the showdown) has paired with anything on the board and you are playing your highest card. Obviously, the highest card in your hand is up against the highest card in an opponent's hand in a showdown and the higher card wins the pot. If, however, the five cards on the board are all higher than the 'hole' cards of each player then it is a split pot.

How to use this book
Read before you leap

Throughout the book you will find a number of diagrams and charts that illustrate what is going on. The following notes will help you decipher the code!

Card diagrams

Some diagrams show a row of cards; some are shaded but the more prominent cards are relevant to the point under discussion.

Table diagrams

All the players are numbered around the table marking where they are sitting in relation to the action. In front of each player is a small circle containing a number that represents the size of the bet by that player. The following symbols represent certain features:

D Dealer   SB Small Blind   BB Big Blind   F Fold

Suits and face cards

Suits are determined by symbols – A ♥ = Ace of Hearts; and K ♣ = King of Clubs, etc.

CLUBS

SPADES

DIAMONDS

HEARTS

A ACE

K KING

Q QUEEN

J JACK

How to play
No Limit Texas Hold'em

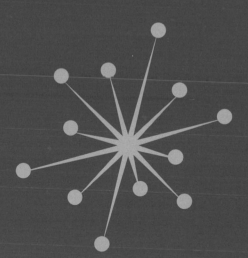

The aim of the game
Learning the ropes

Like love and war, the basic aim of No Limit Texas Hold'em is to win. And to win in this game you need to acquire all your opponents' assets; in other words, you want to win your opponents' chips.

There are two ways to win chips. The first is by making the best five-card hand using your two hole cards (see page 24) and the five community cards available to you. The second way to win is to make your opponents *believe* you are holding a stronger hand than them and force them to fold so you can win the hand uncontested. The 'best' hand is determined according to the hierarchy of hands (see page 16).

How many players?

The game can be played with between two and ten people per table using a single deck of cards.

Chips

In poker games, especially in casinos, chips are substituted for cash. Tournament chips have no monetary value and it is up to the organizer of the event to determine how many chips to allocate at the beginning of each tournament.

Choose the dealer

To nominate the first dealer a single card is dealt clockwise and face up to each player. The player who is dealt the highest-ranking card (Aces high) is nominated the dealer and will deal the first hand. In the event of a tie, suit rankings will decide (Spades, Hearts, Diamonds and then Clubs). After each hand the deal moves clockwise one position around the table.

Ante up (blinds)

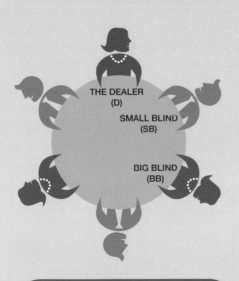

THE DEALER (D)

SMALL BLIND (SB)

BIG BLIND (BB)

Whether a cash game or a tournament there are always compulsory antes/blinds to post each round to guarantee that there is some money in the pot each deal.

The first position seated to the left of the dealer is known as the Small Blind (SB). This is the first player to be dealt cards as the dealer will always deal in clockwise order. The Small Blind is forced to make a compulsory bet. This is known as 'posting' a blind. It is half the size of a full bet.

The first position seated to the left of the Small Blind is known as the Big Blind (BB). The Big Blind also has to make a compulsory bet, double the Small Blind.

In tournaments the blind levels increase in equal time increments. In cash games, however, the blind levels remain the same throughout and only change on the size of game being played.

Towards the end of a tournament an ante (an agreed nominal bet required from each player before the start of a hand) may be introduced on top of the blinds. This means that every player is required to post their ante regardless of whether they actually wish to participate in the hand.

Sample blind structure

Level	SB	BB	Ante	Time
Level 1	25	50		20 mins
Level 2	50	100		20 mins
Level 3	75	150		20 mins
Level 4	100	200	50	20 mins
Level 5	200	400	100	20 mins

Playing the game
Girl gamers get going

It is customary for the person to the left of the dealer to shuffle the deck, then pass the cards to the person to the right of the dealer to cut the deck. This is done to avoid any cheating or collusion.

To ensure that no one deals unscrupulously from the bottom of the deck and to ensure that the bottom card is not exposed, a postillion (cut card) is placed at the bottom. Normally made of brightly coloured plastic, the postillion is the same size as a regular card.

Dealing

1 In No Limit Texas Hold'em the dealer will deal clockwise two cards face down to each player. These cards are known as the hole cards and are only known to the individual player.

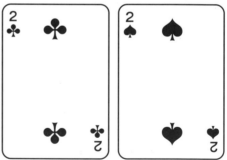

EXAMPLE OF HOLE CARDS

The action

The first seated player after the BB is now first to act. They have the option to post the blind (call), raise or fold. This option moves clockwise around the table until all active players have the same amount in the pot.

 If at any time any person decides to bet (raise the pot), each subsequent player must match this bet (known as calling) or they must fold. Each player must match the action of the preceding player or they are forced to fold. You always have the opportunity to raise when it is your turn.

Call: Match the largest bet previously made. By calling you are staying in the hand and are contributing to the pot.

Raise: Increase the bet when it becomes your turn. You may raise the minimum amount of the Big Blind unless it has already been raised, in which case the minimum will be doubling the bet. Since this is No Limit Texas Hold'em you may raise as much as you like.

Re-raise: This when there has been a raise but another player decides to raise again. There is no limit on the number of raises that are allowed.

Fold: Also known as passing. Folding means you do not wish to continue in the hand and you are discarding your cards. This is done by passing them to the dealer face down who will place them in the 'muck' (discarded cards or pile of cards).

Check: If it comes around to the Big Blind and no one has raised, the Big Blind has the option to check (to refrain from betting). This is because the amount they have already posted is equal to the other players. It is important to note that the Big Blind may also raise.

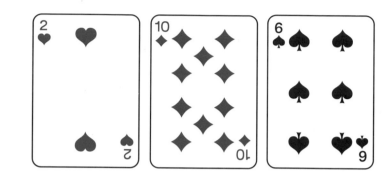

THE FLOP

Open house

Dealing the flop: The dealer now discards the top card of the deck face down. This is known as the burn card. The dealer now deals three cards face up in the middle of the table – these cards are known as the flop and are community cards.

The players must now use their own two hole cards and combine these with the flop to try and make the best hand possible, then bet accordingly.

After the flop has been dealt the action begins again with the Small Blind who has the option to check or bet. This option moves in a clockwise direction until each player has acted. Remember that if at any time any player bets, each subsequent player must match or increase the bet or they must fold. This continues until all players have bet the same amount or folded. If all players simply check then the next card will be dealt.

In this example **Player 1** has made a bet of two. **Player 2** has re-raised and made the bet four.

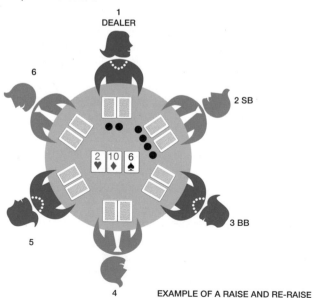

EXAMPLE OF A RAISE AND RE-RAISE

  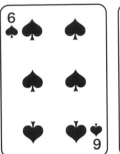 

THE TURN

The turn

4 After each player has acted and all bets have been made, another card is burned and the next card which is dealt face up is known as the turn (or Fourth Street). Again, action begins with the Small Blind, and continues in a clockwise direction. A round of checking or betting occurs until all players have acted and matched the preceding player's action or folded.

THE RIVER

The river

5 After each player has acted and all bets have been made, another card is burned and the next card, which is dealt face up, is known as the river (or Fifth Street). Now the final round of betting takes place, again beginning with the Small Blind and continuing in a clockwise direction.

The showdown

6 Once all bets have been made and matched, the hole cards of each player still involved in the action are revealed face up for all to see and the player with the highest-ranking hand scoops the pot. This is known as the showdown.

In this instance two players are still involved in the pot. **Player 1** has made three of a kind (twos), while **Player 2** is holding a pair of Kings. **Player 1** wins the pot as this hand ranks higher on the list (see page 18).

In the event of a tie, the players involved share the chips equally. In poker games suit rankings (Spades, Hearts, Diamonds or Clubs) do not count and only poker-hand ranks matter. Obviously, the highest-ranking hand claims the pot and if there are any side pots these are also distributed to the respective winners.

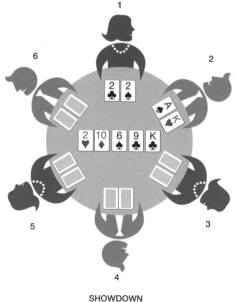

SHOWDOWN

Factbox: Know your terms

Bet/Raise	To put money/chips into a pot that is more than the previous active player.
Big Blind	An early compulsory bet, usually double the Small Blind, seated directly to the left of the Small Blind.
Button	A plastic token placed in front of the player sitting in the nominal dealer's seat. If a house dealer is used, the button rotates clockwise around the table so that each player has the opportunity to be the last to act.
Call	To put the minimum amount of money/chips into a pot to continue playing.
Check	To make no bet when it is legal to do so and thus pass on the action to the next player.
Dealer	The person in charge of dealing the hole cards, dealing the community cards and awarding the pot at the end of the hand.
Flop	The first three community cards dealt simultaneously and face up.
Fold	To not call a bet and thus drop out of the hand.
Hole Cards	The two cards dealt individually to each player face down.
Muck	To throw one's cards into the muck, thereby folding.
Postillion	The plastic card placed at the bottom of the pack by the dealer to prevent anyone seeing the bottom card.
River	The last community card dealt in a hand.
Showdown	The stage at the end of the hand where all active players reveal their cards and the pot is awarded.
Small Blind	Sitting directly to the left of the dealer and bets half the amount of the Big Blind as a compulsory bet.
Turn	The fourth community card dealt, also known as the Fourth Street.

What happens…?
Ask me!

You are the new girl at the table and things can go wrong or seem a bit confusing. Here are some answers to a few of the questions and situations that might pop up.

…if there is a misdeal?

Mistakes happen from time to time. A card might be exposed or somebody might be dealt three cards by mistake. Depending on where you are playing the rules do vary. Normally, the deck will be reshuffled and redealt. If a damaged card is discovered, use a new deck immediately.

…in the event of a tie?

When the conclusion results in a tie, the pot is divided equally. If there is an uneven amount the extra chip goes to the player nearest the dealer's left.

…if there is an all-in and other players involved still have chips?

If a player is all-in (puts all her money in the pot) and other players are still involved, betting continues in a side pot. It is only possible for players to win pots to which they have contributed chips. When showdown occurs and the all-in player wins the main pot, the player with the second-best hand will win the side pot.

How much can I lose?

It is only possible to lose the chips you have in front of you. You may not rebuy chips in the middle of a hand.

At showdown my opponent shows a better hand – do I have to show?

Rules vary from place to place but normally the player who was last to raise is obliged to show her hand first – if this beats what you are holding, normally you can muck your hand without showing. However, other players have the right to ask to see your hand if there is suspected cheating. In some places you are not allowed to muck but must show the table what you were betting with.

Cards speak

In most casinos and card-rooms there is an unofficial rule that 'cards speak'. This means that the hand that is actually the best wins the hand and not a 'claimed' hand. For example, if a player claims a straight and the other player claims two pairs and upon inspection of the cards the straight was erroneously claimed, the two pairs would win the round. There is no other penalty or fine for misclaiming a hand.

If a player 'mucks' her hand into the pile of discarded cards it is generally considered 'dead' and cannot be reclaimed from the 'muck'.

Protect your hand!

It is critical to note that each player is responsible for safeguarding her own cards. Even if the professional dealer was to take your active cards and muck them by mistake, your hand would be dead. Most players place some form of chip or 'lucky charm' on top of their cards to protect them.

Tournament play

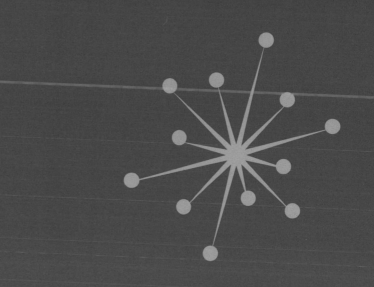

Different types of tournaments

Knowing your freeze-out from your sit 'n go

Just as every girl has her own style, tournaments have their own kind of style and structure. Familiarize yourself with the various permutations until you find one that suits *your* style of play. More important, however, is to discover which one you are best at and makes you the most profit or return on investment (ROI).

The buy-in for each type of tournament depends on the tournament and the casino. Seek a level that is within your means; you want to play where poker is a fun, social activity and does not become a financial burden. Most casinos offer tournaments that range from $10 buy-ins all the way up to the thousands. Online, buy-ins start for as little as a $1!

Freeze-out

Freeze-out is not a treatment you mete out to an erring boyfriend, but a kind of poker tournament that 'freezes out' players after an initial buy-in. You start the tournament on a level playing field with other players and with equal chips. Once you lose your chips you are out of the tournament and there is no option to get back in.

This type of tournament suits players with limited budgets or those who only wish to stake a certain amount in any given game. It is also useful to know you are battling on a level playing field against the other players and the fact that Bill Gates might be seated at your table gives him no financial advantage over you.

Re-buy

This kind of tournament can be very expensive and hazardous, and should be entered with extreme caution. Needless to say, this type is not recommended for beginners. A re-buy allows you to re-buy chips as often as you like once you have lost your initial starting stack. The re-buy period lasts about an hour, after which the tournament becomes a 'freeze-out'.

The major problem with this type of tournament is that people play very loosely and tend to gamble more because they have the option of getting back in the game each time they lose. The other drawback is that you don't know how rich or foolish the person might be sitting next to you. You will notice a marked change in people's style of play after the 'freeze-out' period kicks in.

The major advantage to a re-buy tournament is that it boosts the prize-pool and can be great value if you don't have to re-buy too many times.

Sit 'n Go

Not a new shampoo or hair colour, this tournament format is normally a one-table freeze-out. Sit 'n Go is quick and fun to play and provides lots of opportunities to practise your final table strategies and your God-given talents as a woman. In a ten-seater game, the top three players will normally win the prize-pool proportionately (50-30-20 per cent).

Advantages and disadvantages of different types of tournaments

	ADVANTAGES	DISADVANTAGES
FREEZE-OUTS (MULTI-TABLE)	Great ROI, less gambling and more skill	One bad bet and you could be out
RE-BUYS (MULTI-TABLE)	Greater ROI, larger prize-pools due to extra money	Can be expensive if made to gamble too often
SIT 'N GO	Quick to play, increases skills for final table	Much lower ROI

Tournament mechanics
Learning how to make it work for you

Tournaments are a great way to learn the game at relatively little cost, since you are only liable for the initial buy-in. Buy-ins can range from as little as $1 online and from about $10 in a casino. Depending on the number of players, making money in these tournaments can be a great return on your investment.

Do you want it safe, risky or quick?

Once you have decided which tournament to play in, you pay the entry fee plus a registration fee (normally 10 per cent), which goes to the house. You will be assigned a random seat number (for example, Table 10 Seat 3) and given the same amount of chips as your fellow players. Depending on the type of tournament (re-buy or freeze-out), you may be allowed to purchase more chips during the tournament.

Musical poker chairs

As players are eliminated the tournament director moves players around to keep the tables balanced. Typically, the next person to become the Big Blind will be moved. This ensures that everyone is playing on an even playing field. It wouldn't be fair to have one table of three players and another with ten as the blinds would come around more frequently to the emptier table.

The blinds in a tournament start low and increase as the game goes on. It is always important to be aware of how many players are left in the game so that you stay ahead of the average chip stack.

Avoiding the bubble

When all the money has been counted the prizes will be announced. If the top ten in the tournament are being paid prize money then the eleventh spot is known as the bubble. This has nothing to do with gum and everything to do with disappointment. Most players dread going out in this place because it means they so nearly made the money. As the bubble approaches you will notice the style of play changes dramatically and decisions are harder to make.

Making the final cut

When play gets down to nine or ten players, the final table is created and strategies begin to change again. As players get knocked out, starting hands do not need to be so strong since the odds of someone having a premium hand are reduced. Single table tournaments are a good way to practise final table play. When only two players are left, this is known as heads-up. The winner is the player who ends up with all the chips.

Keeping an eye on the chips

Not the French fries but the chip stacks in front of every player – it is important to be aware of the chip stacks around you at the final table. If someone is sitting with less than three Big Blinds she is probably going to make a move and go all-in with practically anything.

Top tips for winning tournaments

Survive and conquer

Tournaments are all about survival. You will need to use different techniques and the ability to change gears in the middle of the game, something our sex can do to perfection.

* Do your homework. Practise and prepare beforehand. Think about how you will play in the first levels or how much of your stack you are prepared to gamble.

* Get your beauty sleep. Go in refreshed with a clear head. If you are not feeling on top form you will not be making the right decisions.

* Focus. Good concentration is important and even if you are not involved in a hand ensure you are following the rest of the table. Try to guess what people are holding by the way they bet.

* Never be afraid to lose or you will never win. There is always an element of risk and this is a good thing. Be prepared to gamble.

* Avoid getting short-stacked and being blinded off. This puts you in a very vulnerable situation and you will end up going all-in with a weak hand. Other players will be trying to eliminate you because you are weak.

* Be aggressive. It will surprise some of your male opponents, which is good. Better to be in control and lead the betting. Your opponents will know not to bully you.

* Never call a hand that you wouldn't call a raise.

* Never show your cards or tell the table what you had. A girl needs some secrets. Why give away free information. If they want to know, make them pay!

* Avoid slow playing big hands – it will only end in disaster.

* Avoid the big stacks unless you have a monster hand.

* Keep your feminine mystique by having a set routine before folding, calling or raising any hand in order to avoid giving off tells.

* As the flop comes down watch the other players' reactions not the cards.

* Women tend to be good listeners. Use this to your advantage and be attentive to the table chat.

* Always be aware of your table position before playing a hand. In early position make sure your hand is strong in case the pot is raised.

* While the blinds are small, when the Big Blind is only about 5 per cent of your stack, you can afford to play normal poker. When the percentage decreases you will have to start taking more risks.

* Avoid confrontations with the chip leaders without a premium hand.

* Don't develop bad habits that others can pick up on.

* Be aware of how many chips are in play so you can measure your stack accordingly.

* Avoid excessive alcohol at the table. It will affect your decisions.

* Remember anyone can win. Respect your fellow players but fear none of them!

Tournaments or cash games?

Choose the stage to suit your talents

There are marked differences between how you play a tournament and a cash game – try them both to see which suits your style and temperament.

Chip values

In cash games the value of your chips is the same as real money. The blinds stay at the same level and you choose which game you want to play. Always stay within your limit otherwise you will find that your decisions are not based on your cards but on what's left in your wallet.

Time is money

As the blinds are fixed in a cash game, you aren't pressured to find a hand and go with it the way you are in a tournament. Patience will normally pay off. In cash games your time is your own. You are not committed for any longer than you want to sit at the table.

Skills and strategy

Tournaments require two sets of skills, something women find easy to deploy. Firstly, you need the skill of the game and secondly, the skill to adapt to changing circumstances, at which women excel. Tournaments are all about survival whereas in a cash game you play to win more than you lose. In tournaments you can't just play based on the pot odds as you will get knocked out – there are too many other factors to consider. In cash games if you lose you can just reload your stack.

Size does matter

Stack size in a tournament is very important as it marks your position in the game. In a cash game it is relatively irrelevant as long as you have enough in front of you to make proper-sized bets and raises.

Watch and learn

Before you join a cash table, observe the play for a while whether it is online or live. Get to know your opponents before they get to know you. Position is important when selecting your starting hands.

Money, money, money!

Playing cash requires a larger bankroll than a tournament. There is no limit to the amount you can win or lose so keep track of profits and losses.

In a tournament you have to outlast 90 per cent of the field to be a winner. In a cash game it can take only one hand. It is not so important to steal the blinds in cash games as you are not fighting for survival but you actually want to get paid off on a hand.

Tournaments give better rewards for the money invested and there is less risk. However, luck plays a bigger role in tournaments, which is a disadvantage to better players.

Women-only tournaments
Girls' night out

Ladies-only tournaments are the answer to a shy girl's prayer. Poker is a male-dominated game and female players are in the minority, although this is changing. Many women, especially beginners, feel intimidated sitting down to an all-male table, and if you feel unwelcome or out of place it can ruin your evening!

In the last few years ladies-only tournaments have sprung up all over the world and there is a ladies-only event at the World Series of Poker. In spite of how it might look, the point is not to exclude men, but to try to get more women involved in poker. Inexpensive tournaments are a great way to create interest and make women feel more comfortable in competition.

Gain confidence then enter the fray

These tournaments help women gain confidence playing poker, and allow them to feel more comfortable when they play against men. At the moment less than 10 per cent of a tournament field will be made up of women.

Cultivate your girly side

Poker is a competitive sport that anyone of legal age can play. What makes a good poker player has nothing to do with physique (strength, weight, height or speed) but more important factors such as knowledge of the game, concentration, patience, timing, good money management, attitude and discipline, all of which come from the brain. And we girls have these attributes in spades, shall we say!

Brain over brawn every time

Men are naturally the more aggressive sex and this shows in the way they play poker. Use this knowledge and adjust your game to trap them. When playing against other women it normally isn't about ego but plain skill and we don't get so upset if we are made to fold our hands and are outplayed.

Women are much more patient than men by nature and this helps hugely in poker. Playing women-only tournaments can be a lengthy process due to the slow thinning of the field as we women sit back and take it slow.

Practise, practise, practise

As in most sports, practice is very important, and there are many things you can do to practise your poker game. You can study the game and your opponents by making notes. There are numerous books on the market that discuss various strategies. Discuss how you played some hands with fellow enthusiasts – it is always interesting to get a different perspective. And, above all keep playing!

Basic strategy

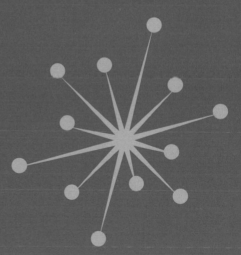

Premium starting hands
Simply the best!

There are four hands (hole cards) in No Limit Texas Hold'em considered to be premium starting hands. These holdings can be played from any position around the table and you should raise and sometimes re-raise to ensure maximum gain to your chip stack.

Four premium hands

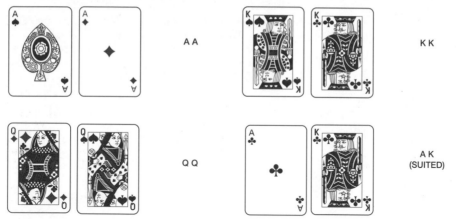

A A

K K

Q Q

A K
(SUITED)

These gems don't come along very often, perhaps once every 60 hands or so. If you are the lucky girl, stay calm and bet strongly pre-flop to get yourself up against one opponent heads-up (two players), as statistically you are more likely to win the pot. Allowing too many other players to limp along with marginal holdings allows too many hands that might beat you. Having your Aces 'cracked' in this game means that your opponent manages to outdraw and beat you, and often it is because the hand was played incorrectly. As far as percentages go, your pair of Aces in the hole will lose about 20 per cent of the time.

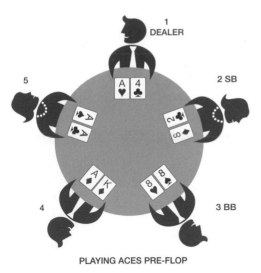

You are **Player 5** and are holding A♣ A ♠.
Player 4 moves first and makes a raise
holding A K ♦. Another player might want
to get involved with a marginal hand so
make a re-raise to isolate **Player 4**. The
action folds around to **Player 3** who is in
the Big Blind. With a raise and a re-raise
already in action it is sensible for her to fold
her pair of 8s. This leaves **Player 4** with the
A K ♦ to call your raise and see the flop.

PLAYING ACES PRE-FLOP

Second tier premium hands

The following starting hands, although second-tier premium hands, are very playable.
Playing these cards is dependent on a number of factors such as position, the number of
players already involved in the pot and the general types of player you are playing against.

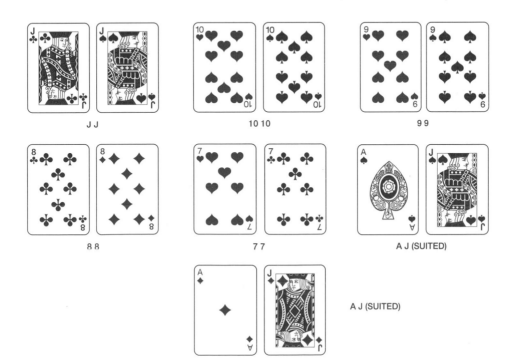

J J

10 10

9 9

8 8

7 7

A J (SUITED)

A J (SUITED)

Weak kicker trouble
Tall, dark, but not very handsome!

As in life, so in cards – sometimes a girl gets stuck with a difficult set of circumstances. In poker, weak kicker trouble means you have perhaps been dealt an Ace or a King but your second card (kicker) is very low. If the board comes down pairing your top card and there is a raise, you will probably lose as your second card will let you down.

Let's take a look at how it might pan out in the diagrams below.

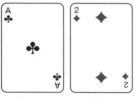

YOU A ♣ 2 ♦

YOUR OPPONENT A ♦ K ♥

BOARD A ♠ Q ♥ J ♦ 8 ♠ 5 ♣

Your opponent wins with a pair of Aces and a King kicker. You are holding a pair of Aces and using the Queen as your kicker, so you lose.

Look on the bright side

There are times where it is right to raise with a hand like this as you are probably winning; for example, if you are in late position and everyone has folded and you are holding a Ace. You only have to beat the blinds and there is every chance your Ace high is winning, so it's best to take down the pot then and there. However, always assess the situation and look for tells.

Cut your losses

If the pot has been raised before it is your turn to act, it is normally best to throw away your hand unless a player has gone all-in and there is very little for you to call. For example, if you are sitting in late position and the blinds are 200–400 and a player goes all-in for 800, it is a good time to call if you are well stacked. They could be making a move with a weak hand or even with just two picture cards.

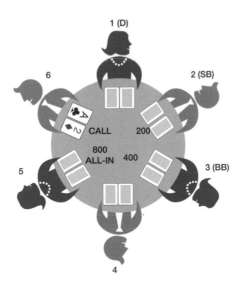

Watch your back

In tournaments you will notice that some players always try to defend their blinds, so be careful who you decide to raise – they may well make a re-raise at you, sensing weakness.

What's your favourite position?
Sitting pretty. Where else?

Position is everything in No Limit Texas Hold'em and it is important to understand why. Learn to use the value of position and it will help you immeasurably.

The best position at the table is the button. You will learn through experience that the single most advantageous thing about playing poker is position and is so critical that it may even outweigh getting good cards.

Hitting the B-spot

Being 'on the button', as it is referred to in poker parlance, means that you are the notional dealer and therefore last to act. The advantages of this happy state of affairs are numerous and a few are outlined below:

* You are last to act.
* You have not committed any blinds or monies to the pot.
* You get to see everyone else's action and moves.
* If everyone folds, you can bully the blinds.
* You are furthest away from posting the blinds.

Now let's explore each of the above and apply them to a game situation.

You are last to act Obviously, this is advantageous because you get to see how strong everyone else is (or pretends to be) and act accordingly. In the latter stages of a tournament when blinds are large, most people will fold before you and you only have to take on the blinds. Lucky you! Since you have a choice you can either play or fold – the blinds are forced to play their cards and if you have a strong or medium hand you can force them off their blinds (make them fold) without even seeing a flop.

You haven't committed any monies to the pot so you can get away cheaply depending on what everyone else does. Your money is safe to bet with later on.

You see everyone else's moves so you are in a position to fold if you feel you are behind regardless of holding a strong hand.

If everyone folds you can bully the blinds by acting strong – they can only call you with a strong hand.

Being furthest from the blinds means that you get to see six to eight more hands before you are obliged to commit any monies to the pot. This is critical in the latter stages of the tournament as people drop like flies and every position gets you closer to taking the pot.

Examples of playing out of position

* If you pick up a suited Ace in first position and flat-call, chances are that there will be a raise. You may well have to lay down your hand as it is unlikely to be winning. Only play very strong hands in the first couple of positions – if you have a pair of Kings or Aces by all means flat-call, as you are praying the pot gets raised so you can re-raise and isolate just one player.

* Playing weak cards in late position is fine if there have been no raises – you are very likely ahead before the flop.

* In heads-up, the first person to act changes position after the turn card is dealt – this is important to recognize in heads-up strategy.

Playing tight
Buckle up!

This doesn't mean playing under the influence of alcohol, which of course no self-respecting girl player will do either! Nor being tight-fisted with your money. No, this is a phenomenon you will notice among novice players of both sexes who, through lack of experience, adopt a 'tight' strategy when it comes to playing poker.

This means that the novice only plays on strong hands or plays fewer hands than the norm, and makes for a bit of a dull game. This is a very understandable strategy and being a novice, she (or maybe he) has not as yet mastered the skills of bluffing or using aggressive play.

Therefore, for a novice, playing A K or A Q, is much easier than playing 9 10 off-suit. The risks in playing premium hands are reduced and the comfort of a strong Ace or King lends security.

Advantages

* You only call with playable premium hands.
* You only raise with premium hands.
* You never really risk your whole stack.
* You signal to the other players that you only play strong hands.
* You probably won't get re-raised.

Loosen up!

The problem with playing a too 'tight game' is that unless you are getting good cards – which of course is hit or miss – your chip stack is constantly being eroded. Another problem is that if other players on your table use their feminine intuition, they will realize this and use it against you. They could trap you and wait for you to get a hand. Worse still, they will automatically fold every time it appears you have a hand and thus you will get even less value.

Disadvantages

* You are eroding your chips waiting for a hand.
* You scare people off and do not get value when you bet.
* You could get trapped.
* You may not get enough good hands to play too tightly.
* You are not adapting your strategy to suit your opponents.

Note that if you project this image at the table, it will be much easier for you to pull off a bluff when the time is right because no one will assume you are making one. So shy and retiring can sometimes work to your advantage. Use with care, like all your feminine wiles!

Playing aggressively
Who's the daddy? (I mean mummy!)

Playing 'tight' probably comes easily to novice players. Playing aggressively must be one of the most difficult strategies for a beginner to pull off. In poker terms playing 'aggressively' means betting without a strong hand.

The easiest type of strategy or game plan for a novice or fairly new player to adopt at the poker table is that of a 'tight' player – it is very difficult to go wrong if your starting hand is a pair or a very strong Ace. Being aggressive with A A or K K is easy but is much more difficult to pull off with 6 10. But we girls are up for a bit of acting!

And the Oscar for best actress goes to...

Aggression, like bluffing, is a skill you develop after months and even years of playing and is honed by practising endlessly. Perhaps not a good idea experimenting with your boyfriend on this one... Watch some of the poker programmes on TV so you can see how the professionals do it.

Stake and chips

Aggressive play involves staking a greater portion of your chips than other players might per hand. It makes sense to proceed with caution if you are a new girl as any errors will cost you more chips than if you were passive. And errors have a nasty habit of bringing on an earlier than anticipated exit, not something a would-be poker starlet wants to have happen.

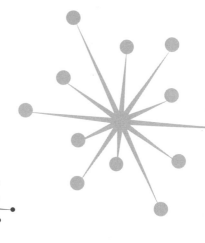

Bluff and double-bluff

By playing a mostly tight style of game like a novice, the scope is there for you to be aggressive with some pots and 'steal' them without the worry of a showdown. Use occasional aggression; adopting an aggressive style in between a tight game-style will help you maintain and hopefully build your chip stack while you wait for premium hands.

Pussycat or tiger – keep them guessing

* Make an occasional re-raise to show the tiger in you.
* Raise with frequency.
* When you are involved in a pot make your opponents pay to catch their cards if you think they are on a draw.
* Bet heavily to get your opponent to make a decision – very few hands are worth going out of a tournament.

Intermediate strategy

Making the most of what you've got

Give me some action!

You have been dealt a hand you like, so what are you going to do about it? You don't want to over-commit your chips if you are going to have to fold by the river. But you want to get maximum value. It's vital to learn how to strike a balance between getting value and risking your chips.

Building your nest-egg

HOLE CARDS

1 First things first – you raise pre-flop to start building the pot. Imagine you've got an A K off-suit (cards of different suits). This is one of the premium starting hands as discussed earlier. Raise to make sure that your opponents call with decent hands and to stop any limpers from seeing the flop cheaply and possibly outdrawing you. A raise here of about three times the Big Blind would be adequate.

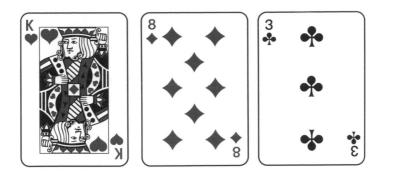

THE FLOP

2 Let's say the flop comes down K 8 3 rainbow (a flop with three different suits). You now hold the top pair with the top kicker and you need to find out the strength of your opponents' hands. This is a very straightforward play and involves no bluffing or deception. Raise again, perhaps half the size of the pot, and see who calls. There are a few hands that could beat you and you need to find out if anyone is holding them.

3 It is possible that someone calls your raise with a pair and hits her set on the flop – this is very hard to read as she is likely to be trapping you. Or someone calls your raise with a weak King and has caught two pairs. This is a potential disaster. You are trying to stop someone who has called with a weak King and is waiting to catch a second pair. By placing a bet you make her pay to see it, while the odds are still in your favour as you currently hold the best hand.

4 You also make a bet in case someone has only hit the bottom pair (3) and you prevent them from seeing another card for free. Always make your opponent make a decision. Be aware that someone could be holding a monster (a very big hand) and is waiting to make a move on you at the river. They could have a massive pair of Aces in the hole and you just didn't see it coming!

Tournament tactics –
early stages
Warmed up and ready for action!

In tournaments the main objective is to win all the chips and be the victor. To get to that final table and scoop the prizes you need to have a plan – big money is at stake but the winning strategy is very different from playing a straight cash game.

Hot tips for cool play

Keep it tight In the early stages the blinds are very small in relation to your stack. Play tight to avoid being eliminated.

Chinks in the armour Some players will be aggressive. Keep a note of these players and find a hand to trap them.

Spend or save? If re-buys are allowed in the early stages prepare yourself for loose play. Decide in advance if you want to invest in a re-buy or two and play accordingly.

Don't risk your assets As blinds are low you can play marginal hands such as suited connectors (consecutive cards of the same suit) and small pairs but do not risk more than 5 per cent of your stack. You could hit big on the flop and be headed for a double-up (doubling your money with an all-in).

Hiding the goodies It can be advantageous to play your premium hands conservatively before the flop to minimize big losses after the flop. If you do flop a massive hand it will be much easier to disguise and get more value from it.

A bit of rough If you like to be aggressive, use the early stages to build a substantial stack. You will be putting your tournament life at risk but if it works it will put you in a better position to win. It allows you to weather the storms as you will have chips left over.

Playing it shy and retiring The best strategy for a passive player is to aim for a steady accumulation of chips. Try and see a lot of hands at a cheap price and take small pots here and there.

No nasty stuff Don't worry about eliminating other players at this stage.

Well-stacked Keep your stack above the average. This will normally be displayed on the tournament clock.

Eye up the opposition If you manage to acquire a big stack do not get into confrontations with similar stack sizes – focus your attention on those who are weak.

Tournament tactics – middle stages

Firming up your position

The middle stages of a tournament call for a change in play due to rising blinds and diminishing chip stacks.

Keep your baby blues on these

Stealing the blinds As the blinds increase they represent an increasing percentage of the average stack. So winning the blinds becomes more significant and the first player to enter the pot will probably raise rather than call in the hope of stealing the blinds.

Nothing ventured... It will now cost you a significant proportion of your stack to call the raise so be careful if you limp into a pot.

Nothing gained There may be a lot of pre-flop raising and folding, so seeing a flop becomes rarer.

Quick off the mark As you near the final table the number of players at each table decreases to keep tables even. Blinds will come around fast and furious, so should be factored into your play. Use more aggression, girl, especially in late position.

Fast and loose Loosen up your starting hand requirements for an opening raise.

Tight response Tighten up your calling hands to a raise from an opponent.

Freebies Every time you win a set of blinds you are buying another round in which to see free cards.

Handy work Your objective should be to win a hand per round to combat the increasing blinds.

Survival of the fittest The longer you survive the greater your chances of hitting a premium hand.

Size does matter Bigger stacks will command more respect and will often win hands unopposed. Smaller stacks get called more often as the risk will not damage the big stacks.

High-rise A raise at this point should be about six times the Big Blind.

Change tactics If you find yourself short-stacked, change your strategy. You cannot limp or raise with a marginal hand – you will be called. Any Ace or low pair is enough to go all-in and hope to be doubled up.

Eliminate the weak Experienced players with big stacks will often call a short stack all-in even if they have a poor hand. They risk a few chips for the chance to move one spot nearer the money.

Check down Be prepared to check down a hand (pass on the action) if another player is all-in. Do this to double the chance of the short stack going out. The correct etiquette is a small bet if you have the nuts (an unbeatable hand).

Tournament tactics – final stages

A glimpse of the glittering prizes

If all has gone to plan and you have survived up to this point, you are almost within reach of all that delicious prize money. But keep your cool and watch everyone else with a beady eye.

Watch out

Big bucks Blinds will be so high that all players will be concerned about them.

In with a chance Keep an eye on the number of players left and how many remain until the prize money kicks in.

Yours is bigger than mine Eye up your opponents' chip stacks and try to work out who needs to make an all-in move.

Naughty then nice If you have a large stack the correct strategy is to be very aggressive in raising and very conservative in calling.

Sit back With just a few chips left, tighten up and allow other players to knock themselves out and bring you just into the money. They may want to make a deal (see opposite) to speed up the bubble and add another couple of placings to the money list and you want to be in the game for this.

Let's make a deal

Deals are very common in tournaments when the blinds get so high that lady luck comes into play a lot more. The last few players are allowed to agree a deal to share the prize fund in different proportions to that originally put forward. A lot

of tournaments end in this way because regardless of how big a lead the chip leader has, the blinds are so high that who wins will be more a matter of luck than skill or weight of chips.

It is important to bear in mind that any deal requires the explicit agreement of all the remaining players. If you do not like the proposed deal you do not have to accept it; simply ask the dealer to carry on. If things continue to go your way you will end up with all the chips and the bulk of the prize money. There are three main types of deal.

Saver
All players still in who subsequently get eliminated outside the original prize scale. For example, if there are eight players left and only six prizes then the players may agree that the next two players eliminated will receive a small percentage, which is taken off the first prize. The game then continues.

Complete deal
The whole prize fund is distributed among the remaining players and the game is ended at this point. The amount each player receives will be related to the number of chips they currently have but the exact amount will be subject to negotiation.

Part deal
Part of the prize fund is distributed among the remaining players and then the game continues, normally on the basis that the winner takes all of the remaining prize money and the trophy if there is one. The deal is normally done in relation to current chip stacks.

The big bluff
Putting on a star performance

Bluffing is the art of making a bet with the worst hand, causing your opponent to fold a better one. How good is that? Try some of these when the time is right.

Bluffing is based on an inherent feeling or instinct and could be based on any of the following considerations:

* You know/assume your opponent is weak.
* You know/assume you can make your opponent believe you have a strong hand.
* You know/assume your opponent won't risk his tournament life.
* You think that your opponent considers you a 'rock'.
* You are desperate.
* You are a 'maniac' player or a bully.

Bluffing is a long-term strategy. Just doing it on the first hand and never again during the game is not bluffing – it is just getting lucky.

Semi-bluff and naked bluff

You hold next to nothing (semi-bluff) and do not have a 'made hand'. However, you bet comfortably with the knowledge that even if you get a call you have cards in the deck that can help you; for example, when you have seen the flop you find you have a flush draw and an up-and-down straight draw. In the naked bluff you are exposing yourself if you make this move, but not your physical assets, honey. You make a bet that you pray doesn't get a call because there is nothing in the deck to help you. This is very high risk and should only be attempted if you can put an accurate 'read' on your opponent.

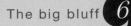

Re-bluff

This is high-adrenaline stuff. If you sense someone is bluffing, then it is time to show him up and re-raise with absolutely nothing. It will be impossible for him to call since he was betting with nothing in the first place.

Delayed bluff

You have sweet nothing in your hand but you flat-called (called a bet without raising) your opponents' raise pre-flop and post-flop; when you come out raising at the end you are representing much larger holdings than it appears you were 'trapping' with.

Positional bluff

You are sitting in late position (betting after almost everyone else because of position) and not many players have entered the pot. There have been no raises so you try to buy the pot right by making a significant raise. The blinds will normally fold and any other player who has already called the blind will be thinking that they will be out of position throughout the hand as you will always be acting after them. Be careful though as this is the most well-known bluff.

Check-raise bluff

You are against one opponent and the first to act, you simply check – the other player may see this as weakness and make a bet. Holding nothing of value you don't fold but pretend strength by re-raising. You might well get him to fold by creating this strong image of your hand. On the other hand he might raise again and you will be forced to fold. Choose your player carefully to make this move.

The cost of bluffing
How much?

Bluffing is a 'strategy' that you should only adopt after you have played several hands and made mental notes on all the other players and their styles of play. Then you will know who to bluff, who not to bluff and hopefully how much to bluff.

Throwing it away

Betting 100 with no hand into a pot of 1,500 is not a good bluff. Equally, betting 1,500 into a pot of 300 is not a good bluff. And finally, betting against the chip leader, if you are in a weak chip position is not a good bluff as they will probably call for the value.

Bluff or double-bluff?

Implicit in a bluff is the fact that you do not have a strong hand and you need to win the pot without a showdown. If you do have a strong hand you will probably not be bluffing, unless, of course, you are feigning weakness in order to attract a bet and trap someone.

Timing is all

Now, assuming that you have a weak hand, the timing and amount of the bluff is critical. Focus on players who are weaker than you and wait for a good table position. Target players you know are playing a 'tight' game. Be aware that your table image will be taken into consideration before your opponents make a call and if you have been playing fairly loosely it is likely you will find a caller.

Watch those pennies

Finally, the amount of the raise has to be enough to deter callers and yet justify winning the pot. Do not bet 1,000 to win a pot of 500. Also, be aware that as you are bluffing and hold no hand, if called, this is the amount you would lose. And 'over-bets' are a signal to other players of your inexperience.

To win a pot of about a 1,000 a bet of 60 per cent should suffice. If your chip stack can justify it, a 100 per cent bet will ward off anyone without a strong hand. But remember you are risking 1,000 to win a 1,000 – make sure your chips, position and reading of the game justifies the move.

Adrenaline rush

Bluffing is one of the most exciting elements of the game and the feeling of pulling off a magnificent bluff is fantastic, but be sure to keep it to yourself or you may find that next time you have an unwanted caller!

Set the trap
Man-hunt!

Trapping is an art in poker and requires huge restraint on your part. A good person to trap is an aggressive player who is continually raising and bullying the table. A trapper under-bets a strong hand to create a larger pot.

How to set your trap
Picture the situation

1 You are sitting in middle position and look down to find a pair of Aces. You have flat-called (called a bet without raising) and the aggressive player is sitting in late position and makes a raise. You flat call the raise and see the flop. Perhaps normally you would re-raise but you are trying to conceal the strength of your hand by not betting out.

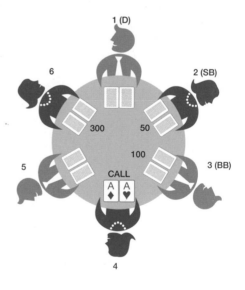

HOW TO SET THE TRAP

THE FLOP

The flop comes down A K 2 rainbow (all different suits). Yippee, that means three Aces for you and you are sitting pretty. But keep your cool.

You have flopped top set – the nuts. You check. Your opponent bets 400. You call.

THE TURN

Here comes the turn. Up comes K ♠. How good is that! You now have a full house – three Aces and two Kings.

The only possible hand out there beating you is quad (four) Kings but as your opponent is betting, this is unlikely. You check and he bets the size of the pot. You re-raise him hoping that he has the King and therefore cannot put down his cards. Got him!

Trapping is a very profitable way of gaining chips but it is all about timing. If your opponent has no hand or is bluffing it will be very easy for him to fold. As at no point during the hand have you initiated the betting he will not take you for holding a pair of Aces!

Learning to fold
Live to fight another game

One quality every brilliant poker player must cultivate is the ability to lay down a big hand. It may hurt but sometimes it is the correct thing to do.

Graceful in defeat

1 You are playing in a tournament and every pot you try to enter has been re-raised and you haven't had a strong enough hand to call all-in. After being card dead for a while you look down and see a glorious pair of Queens and think that it's Christmas!

2 You are sitting in fourth position and the player before you makes a raise. You make a re-raise.

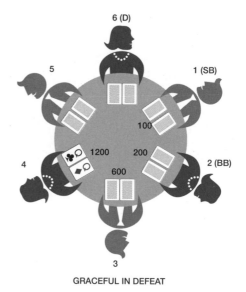

GRACEFUL IN DEFEAT

3 Your opponent now re-raises for all your chips. He has done this once before to someone else and he was holding Aces. What do you do?

4 The answer is fold. It is likely that he is holding Aces again or a pair of Kings. To re-raise with anything less is unlikely. Unless you suspect a bluff, it's time to exit and wait for another hand.

It can be very difficult letting go of a big hand but in a tournament you have to think 'is it worth going out of the tournament for this?'. Most players in this situation don't fold as they just can't do it.

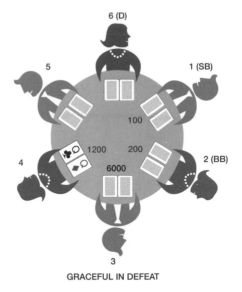

GRACEFUL IN DEFEAT

THE FLOP

If your opponent had just called your raise and the board had come down K 10 6 and he had come out betting for all your chips, you have to believe he has a King or better. At the end of the day, you only have a pair and not even a top pair at that.

Advanced strategy

Playing the short stack
Luckless lass

Being the short stack is not a great position in tournament poker. It's a horrible situation where everything looks gloomy and the light at the end of the tunnel is only the taxi cab waiting to take you home.

The slippery slope

Playing the short stack means you know and fear that each hand you play may be your last – that is, of course, if the blinds don't eat up your stack and eliminate you by default in the interim.

And no, you are not paranoid, because, yes, every player on the table is eyeing up your chips and planning to bully and target *you* before they tackle anyone else on the table.

Coming back from no-man's (or woman's) land

With careful practice and a few basic rules you can learn to manage this situation; with skill and luck you can get yourself out of it and back into a challenging position.

I am a rock

No matter what playing style you prefer in normal circumstances, the 'rock' persona must come to the fore as your stack dwindles. And the closer you are to exiting the more rock-like your game should be.

This is no time to take risks or attempt to bluff your opponents as you will surely be called by someone and without being lucky, you – along with Elvis – will certainly be leaving the building.

Use your position to get ahead

The most important thing in poker – even more than being chip leader perhaps – is position. This should be even more evident than ever when you are low-stacked. Using your position carefully will not only help you win pots but also help you to steal a few despite your limited strength.

Pounce

Being hand selective is the most important factor to consider when your chips are low. As the tournament progresses and blinds are excessive, fewer players will call the Big Blind. The moment you have a strong hand you should pounce. If a player shows or you sense weakness, make your move. There is nothing worse than watching an inexperienced player on the short stack waiting for pocket Aces only to be blinded away before they ever arrive.

Go for it, girl!

Hands such as K Q, K J, Q J or A x (x means that any card below 10 can be referred to as Ace – Rag) are very strong and are worth risking your tournament life on. An advantage to being short-stacked is that when you do go all-in, the other players will assume you have a strong hand since you would not want to risk going out of the tournament on 7 9. Therefore, they will need strong hands themselves to call your bet lest they double you up and create a monster.

Using position and the knowledge that you would only play a strong hand can also allow you to steal a few blinds here and there, but remember that any mistake will be your last.

Tips for Luckless Lass

* Remember that tournaments are frequently won by someone who came back from 'a chip and a chair'. Never give up!
* Do not limp into hands that you will have to fold to a raise.
* Only call an all-in with a very strong hand.
* Look for maximum value when going all-in.
* When less than six times the Big Blind, consider an all-in move with any strong hand to steal the blinds.

Playing a medium chip stack
Miss Average

If you are not in the enviable position of chip leader in a multi-table tournament, then being middle-stacked is a very comfortable place to be indeed. It is like an old pair of jeans that fit well and can always be relied upon.

Stuck in the middle

Holding the average stack in a tournament is a tricky situation. You do not have the pressure to steal the blinds, but on the other hand you do not have the luxury to play speculative hands without big piles of chips in front of you. It becomes a much more conservative game.

Stick to the plan

As a middle-stacked player you have the luxury of sticking to your original game plan and maintaining the style of play that suits you best. There is no need to do anything rash and your chips dictate that you can play the game at a steady pace and wait for your cards and opportunity. As always, the rule to being a successful poker player is patience, position and plays – making the right ones at the right time should ensure victory.

Dealing with the haves and have-nots

The short and big stacks can be fearless due to their chip position. Big stacks have nothing to lose and the short stacks will take gambles. You have the most to lose and the most to gain. You must be extra selective about the hands you play or you will find yourself relegated to the short stack. Don't give the short stacks a chance to double through. The big stacks will treat you with the same caution. When you finally decide to play a hand, play it strong and avoid situations where you will have to back down.

Biding your time

Also remember that as the medium stack you will have on average about 20 times the blinds – this equates to approximately 60 hands, depending on the number of people at the table and the blind levels. This means that you have up to 60 hands to make a move or play a hand, thus patience is the key. Waiting for the correct situation will see your chip stack move to a stronger position. Remember, if you do nothing at all, by virtue of the blinds that need to be posted, other people with shorter stacks will be eliminated before you, bringing you closer to the final table and the money placings.

Rags to riches and vice versa

Remember that you are only one all-in away from either being the short stack or the chip leader. Your next move will either place you in peril or set you up for victory. Be hand selective, although if you have the safety of a medium stack you can bluff if the situation warrants such as strategy action.

Tips for Miss Average

* Be extra hand selective, and when you choose a hand play it strong. Don't waste chips on marginal hands.
* Use your position to steal blinds, especially from weaker players and short stacks directly to your left. Don't double up the short stacks.
* Watch out for the table maniac – the person who calls an all-in with 'any two cards'.
* Exercise patience.

Playing a big chip stack
Top girl!

This is where you want to be – the chip leader. Every player wants to be here, from the minute the tournament starts and most importantly, it's the best position to be in when the tournament ends. As the saying goes, 'he (or she!) who dies with most chips, wins!'.

You call the shots

Striving to become chip leader is desirable on several accounts. First, you secure your position in case of a 'bad beat' (being outdrawn when you have the better hand). Second and more important, it allows you to dictate the game to suit your style, so regardless of the types of players seated at your table, you can play the game and run the show.

Encourage those maniacs

When you have a big stack you welcome the 'maniac' although her game will change and adapt to the situation. Every other player will still play their own game – until they are confronted by you and then you're the boss. The 'maniac' will be a cowering shrinking violet and will avoid you like the plague.

Use your stack

The difference between a good poker player and a true poker professional is best emphasized by how the professional uses her chip-stack advantage to strengthen her position and put herself in a position to claim victory. If a great player has the chip lead she will go on to claim victory. This is not a guarantee for a weaker player in the same situation.

Manipulate and manoeuvre

As the big stack or chip leader you can really manipulate the table and game. The skill is about out-bluffing, out playing and out-manoeuvring your opponents and is best displayed when you have the chips.

Hands that may be considered marginal by most players, become premium hands to the chip leader and premium hands are basically opponent eliminators. Even weak hands played properly will ensure that you maintain or build your stack since the threat of exit from the tournament is a great sword in your arsenal.

Don't become Miss Bossy Boots

Once they become chip leader, amateur players and even some good players make the mistake of becoming the table 'policeman', and giving advice to other players. The smarter players will fold, thus maintaining their own stacks, while encouraging you to call – especially small raises and especially the Small Blind. Do not fall into this trap and play your own game.

Tips for Top Girl

* If you get a healthy chip stack, maintain and increase it.
* Be aggressive and raise regularly.
* Don't feel that you have to call a raise because you are chip leader – you will probably end up doubling up the short stacks and lose your lead.
* Try to eliminate the short-stacked player and don't confront the medium stacks with marginal hands.

The check raise
A crafty move

Perhaps one of the strongest and least anticipated moves in No Limit Texas Hold'em, the check raise is a great move to keep up your sleeve.

Hiding your strength

The check raise happens when you initially check and a player acting after you bets and then you re-raise when the betting comes around to you again. This shows the player that you were masking the strength of your hand. It represents greater strength than raising and calling a re-raise.

When a player raises it is often a speculative bet to find out who else has a good hand, but it may be a bluff or a continuation bet from a pre-flop raise.

Using the check raise
Picture the situation

1 You are dealt a very strong hand, perhaps a pair of Kings or Aces. You are in first position but you don't want to scare anyone off so you flat-call (call a bet without raising) the blinds. A couple of people also flat-call but the player on the button decides to raise.

2 With a big pair, you want to eliminate the other two flat-callers so you re-raise (this should ensure that at least the flat-callers fold and the raiser calls). The original raiser could be on a bluff and fold but at least you have made him commit some chips to the pot.

3 There is a downside to this play – if no one raises you are now up against three other players with no knowledge of their hand strength.

Sometimes you can use the check raise move as a bluff. Just be sure to use it against players who will fold, for example, tight players with weaker hands who won't call you or you raise enough to scare the marginal hands off. You will find that the check raise will eliminate all but the strongest hands.

Reaping the benefits

The benefits of check-raising are simple. You check or flat-call, feigning weakness to encourage a bet so you get extra money in the pot without trying and you will probably be the favourite if they do call. It also slows down aggressive players and they will think twice before putting in a bet if you are still involved in the hand.

Think of your position

Position is important in check-raising – the player you hope will raise is directly on your left. This is so you have a chance to see what everybody does before it is your turn to act. You may well get a few callers before you have to show your own strength. The fewer players between you and the original raiser the better, just in case one of them was planning a check raise of their own.

Knowing the odds
Should I stay or should I go?

In poker there are times when it is correct to call someone's bet or raise because the pot value dictates that you should. Know your odds and it will help.

Pot odds

This is a method of calculating the value of a bet. Pot odds are calculated by dividing the pot by the cost of calling a bet.

If there is $100 in the pot and the bet is $20 then the pot odds would be 5 to1, the amount you can win is worth five times the cost of your bet.

If the odds on you holding the winning hand are shorter than this, say, 4 to 1 or 3 to 1, this represents a good bet. If they are longer, that represents a riskier bet, and poor value, but if they are the same, then it's an even money bet (see chart on page 147).

Implied odds

This is the money you expect to get from an opponent if you make your hand and the betting continues. You need to have a pretty accurate read on your opponent's hand as well as his play. He also needs to have a large enough stack to make it worth your while to speculate.

You guess that your opponent is holding a high pocket pair and the flop gives you a straight draw. It is worth your while staying in the hand to catch one of your outs (see page 86) and therefore make a better hand and take down the pot. Of course, if the raise is so disproportionate to the pot and you are short-stacked it is probably not worth it. This is a key amateur error.

Reverse pot odds

This is the amount it will cost you, and you stand to lose afterwards, by drawing at and making the second-best hand.

Example: You call raises trying to draw to the straight when your opponent already has made their flush.

When calling bets and thinking of the odds always be aware of how it is going to affect your chip stack in the tournament. If you are harbouring a large stack, it is much easier to make these decisions as ultimately it is not going to end your tournament life. If you feel someone is drawing to a very strong hand against you, make the bet large enough so that they do not have the odds to call you.

Counting your outs
Help!

While no one expects you to be a mathematical genius, the knowledge of basic odds and fractions is very useful in poker. I am not talking about illegal card-counting that can get you thrown out of most casinos, but very legal card-counting.

Ins and outs

Knowing your 'outs' (the number of cards left in the deck that will improve your hand) is critical to the game of poker. Now, everyone knows there are 52 cards in a standard deck. These are composed of four suits of Ace, Jack, Queen and King, plus 10 to 2 (13 cards a suit).

Remember that in poker suits do not play and thus a flush vs flush situation is broken by highest card and not by suit and therefore a royal flush in Clubs is the same as a royal flush in Hearts, Diamonds or Spades.

Lucky 13

Anyway, once you realize that there are 13 cards of each suit and four of any value, then, working out your 'outs' in any particular hand is quite easy. Imagine you are **Player 6** (right). Assuming you can see everyone's hand and the four community cards (opposite), how many 'outs' do you have on the river of winning the hand?

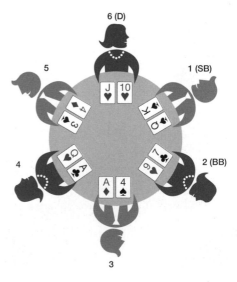

LUCKY 13

THE FLOP   **TURN**

Answer

The answer is 11. Did you get it right?
Two 7s for a straight (note the 7 would
give Player 1 a flush), two Queens for a
straight, 7 hearts for a flush.

So always count your 'out' cards and
obviously, the higher the number of outs
the more chance you will have of hitting
one of them and winning the hand.

Knowing where you stand in the hand

Where am I?

Knowing where you stand in any given hand is critical to your long-term success as a poker player. Without knowing it players will give you signs or 'tells' of their position or strength and it is up to you to ensure that you extract as much information from them as possible.

Subliminal messages

Without even reading this or any other book you will be gathering information, but it is also important to know why, how and when to do it.

You will certainly be doing it each time you raise or bet – these are signs to your opponents that say 'I have a strong hand'. Equally, they are relaying information to you each time they call a bet or raise, saying back to you 'we realize you are strong, but we are strong too' or 'we are bluffing and plan to steal the hand away from you'.

Look for the tell-tale signs

The critical difference between a good poker player and a great poker player is the ability to differentiate between the bets and determine what a player is saying or relaying when she bets, calls or raises. Of course, you never know for sure until a potential showdown, but you should be able to gather some information. There is always a chance that you could be the victim of a bluff but take solace in the fact that on some occasions it will be you who is perpetrating the hoax.

However, in most cases a bet or raise will let you know where you stand. This is especially true of a continuation bet. Either your opponent is pulling one hell of a bluff or she genuinely does have a strong hand and it is time for you to lay down yours and await a better opportunity.

Figuring out where you stand

Picture the situation

1 You are **Player 3** and hold K K. Blinds are 400–800. You raise 2,400 and all but **Player 6** fold. The flop shows A 3 6. Your pre-flop raise has isolated you with just one player as you wanted but that Ace on the flop is worrisome.

2 This is the only card you did not want to see, but did your opponent call you because she was holding an Ace? Chances are anyone calling a large raise such as 3,000 probably has an Ace, but she could just as easily have called with a pair (Q Q, J J, 10 10 etc) if she thought you were raising with A K or A Q. A bad or desperate player may even call with K Q or K J.

3 Now you need to bet to see where you stand. A continuation bet of a further 2,400 will do one of two things: force her to fold since she will assume you did raise with A K, A Q; or if she has a strong Ace she will call or raise. This should be your cue to act like a great player and lay down a monster hand such as K K because there is an Ace on the board.

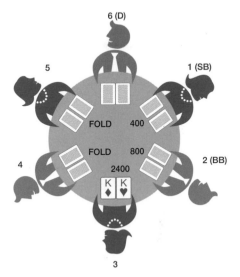

FIGURE OUT WHERE YOU STAND

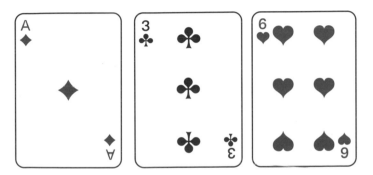

THE FLOP

The continuation bet
Working that semi-bluff

A continuation bet is when the final pre-flop raiser leads out with the betting after the flop comes down.

Take the middle road

Looser, more aggressive players seem to lead out after raising pre-flop. Weaker players rarely make the continuation bet unless they are sure they are winning. This strategy is weak and liable to be exposed by the other players. Players who only bet when they have a hand are very easy to read because they are so predictable.

The key to making good continuation bets is to strike a balance between the two – maybe just over half the time you make a pre-flop raise.

Which one is your type?

There are two types of continuation bets you can make:

1 Make this bet if you are still convinced you are winning and try to build up the pot. For example, you hold a medium pair, say 10s, and the board comes down low. You have an over-pair and are trying to claim the pot then and there.

2 The second type is when you are trying to establish if you are still ahead, so you make a speculative continuation bet to find out where you are in the hand. If you are still holding a pair of 10s but a Jack comes down you will raise to find out if anyone has hit that Jack or perhaps is holding something better.

A good example is when you are representing strength. This could be when you have raised pre-flop holding an A K or A Q. The flop has come down low so you put out a bet even though you only have Ace high. Even if you are called you still have over-cards in which to hopefully improve your hand if needed. You want your opponents to think you are holding a pair and for them to fold even if they have hit the low flop.

Be wary

Always be aware of what else might be out there. If your bet is too small you could allow those with drawing hands in, so be wary of the turn and the river. If the flop hasn't helped you it may well have helped your opponents. Be wary of making speculative continuation bets on a dangerous-looking flop. This is especially important having made a bet pre-flop and attracted a lot of callers. Someone may well be playing a good hand against you.

These types of bets should be made against tight players who won't call you with a weak hand, or passive players who won't re-raise you.

Do I, don't I?

If the flop doesn't improve your hand and looks risky you should avoid making this semi-bluff bet. And if the flop greatly improves it, try slow-playing (bet less than the strength of the hand in order to get more players into the pot and/or deceive other players about the strength of your hand) the hand in order to get maximum value. For example, if you were raising with a pair pre-flop that turns into three of a kind on the flop.

Continuation bets should usually be between 50 and 100 per cent of the pot.

Playing good hands
You've got the nuts!

The best feeling in poker is when you discover you are holding an unbeatable hand, known as the Nuts, and your opponent is betting into you. Stay calm and don't give your opponents any clues!

Playing the nuts hand
Picture the situation

1 You are holding A♥ 3♥. The flop comes down K♥ 10♥ 2♥. Down girl, and keep this pleasure to yourself! The hand is unbeatable. Unless the board pairs by the river you will still be holding the nuts – in this case it is known as the nut flush.

2 How should you play this? You want to extract maximum value, but you don't want to scare anyone off. The only thing you want to know is have they flopped two pairs or three of a kind?

YOU

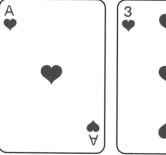

THE FLOP

3 If you are in early position, check and allow someone else to initiate the betting. Flat-call if you think they are weak. If you sense strength maybe re-raise them. If they have hit their set make them pay to draw their full house. The hands you want to draw in are those on straight draws, so if the board looks like it helped someone for that hand, keep them in by betting small. It is very tempting to re-raise and get all your chips in, praying for a call but you will only succeed in scaring them off.

4 The turn is critical. If the board pairs you must raise to find out if that card has helped your opponents. If it hasn't and is another heart you have to hope they are holding a heart or they will get scared.

5 If the river comes down and the board still hasn't paired you have the absolute nuts. If you are first to act, place a small bet – perhaps half the size of the pot – as if you are trying to steal the pot; you might get re-raised if you are lucky. If no other hearts have fallen, your opponent might think you have missed your flush draw and are trying a bluff, which is exactly what you want him to think. You could check but that would allow him to do the same and see your cards for free. Only do this if you are confident of a raise.

The most important thing about holding the nuts is to extract maximum value from it. This is an art and you must not overplay your hand.

Playing drawing hands
Catch me if you can!

Don't attempt this until you've read 'Outs' (pages 86–87) and 'Pot Odds' (page 84). These hands are only good when you actually catch your 'draw', and will make you look very foolish if you don't.

Drawing hands the wrong way...
In the example below you are **Player 1**.

After the flop you not only had a flush draw but also a straight draw. Both of these hands are very strong and sure to be pot winners. However, although you would have called pretty much any raise after the turn, in fact, after the river you end up with only a 7 high. Not really a hand you want to turn over and show everyone. Expensive and fruitless!

The key is to learn how to play these hands to ensure that you get maximum value while avoiding major dents to your chip stack.

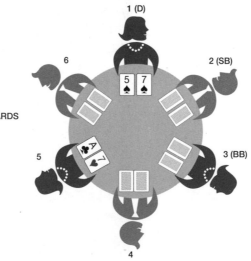

PLAYING DRAWING CARDS

| THE FLOP | THE TURN | THE RIVER |

...and the right way

How could you have played the above hand differently? Using your knowledge of outs you realize that before the river card was dealt you had 17 outs. This is almost as many as you can have holding two random cards and thus worth chasing. With this in mind raise a large amount (maybe even all-in, after the turn, to deter your opponent from calling). A massive raise may alert the others to the fact that you are on a flush draw but they may also think you have a stronger Ace. Either way, it would be difficult for someone holding A 7 to call. This would be the tack of an aggressive player.

However, a steady player would probably play the hand as it transpired and take her medicine. Sometimes you can't win every hand!

See as much as you can

Drawing hands are just that – drawing. Without hitting the right cards, they are meaningless and almost always lose. Therefore, it is wise to see as many cards as cheaply as possible until you hit your draw. If the raise or bet is too steep then let your hand go. Having said that, do not forget all you know about pot odds and outs! Remember, however good your A K looks, it is still a drawing hand.

Changing gears
Everything but reverse

Not in your car, at the poker table! If you watch the pros on television you will notice how they vary their game depending on the situation. This is 'changing gears' and is fundamental to tournament success.

Like sex, but different

In poker there will be times when you should be aggressive, times when you should be passive and times when you should just be. Calculating which tack to employ and when to employ it is the hallmark of a great player.

Styles change

Throughout your game you could use several playing styles (see pages 108–109) but these should be determined once you have assessed your opponents. In the early stages devote some time to sitting back and observing the other players. Determine who is strong and who is weak, who can be bullied and who is a maniac. Once you have assessed the opposition you can now put your own game plan into play.

Keep 'em guessing

No matter what style you employ, it is vital that you deviate from your starting position or change gears in order to win. It throws your opponents off guard but also stops you becoming too predictable. If everyone thinks you're a rock they will continually fold to your bets. Equally, if you a maniac you will continually have showdowns with one or more opponents.

The right style to fit the occasion

Of course the situation at the table may dictate how you play but it is imperative that you know and use different styles. If your chip stack is low then become a rock. If you have a mountain of chips, be the bully. If everyone else is aggressive, be passive and let them knock each other out.

Varying your game will help you take advantage of the table and maximize your chip stack. Play big hands strongly and then play some not so strong hands. Mix up your game so that no one is able to put a read on you.

Keep the end of the road in sight

Remember the object of the game is to cross the finish line in first place and you shouldn't care whether you do it in first or fifth gear.

Avoiding elimination
Bubble trouble

The final person eliminated prior to prize-money placings being awarded is said to occupy the bubble – poker's most unfortunate position.

Avoiding the nasty patch

If you are fortunate enough to still be in a tournament as it draws to the final stages you will note a marked change in your opponents' playing styles as you approach the 'bubble' position. Everyone will be doing their utmost to avoid this humiliation.

After all, no one wants to spend all that time and effort only to be eliminated just before the real party starts. Players will tighten up and often you will see everyone folding to the blinds since no one is keen to risk their chip stacks and end up being sent home without any prize money.

Bring out the bully

By the time the tournament reaches the bubble stage the blinds will have increased to quite a significant amount; this is a great time to take advantage and to try to monopolize the weaker players.

If you are medium-stacked it is an excellent opportunity to be aggressive and rebuild your position. Target weak and tight players and your aggression will be rewarded as the possible fear of missing out on money placings will cause people to fold even quite strong hands.

For short-stacked players, it is all or nothing time so be wary as they may call with weakish hands.

Passive-aggressive

Ironically, it is the chip leader who becomes most passive as she awaits the prospect of a final table; she sits back and bides her time unless she has a monster hand.

The bubble is your cue to change gear and become more aggressive while exercising caution. This might mean changing from a 'rock' to a 'maniac', but it could prove fruitful. Play the predator and prey on your opponent's fears about not making the final table and, at the same time, consolidate your own position and chip stack.

Implementing this strategy in timely fashion will ensure that you never exit any tournament on the bubble and in fact, when you enter the final table, you will be doing so with a healthy chip stack that has been doubled or trebled in the last ten hands of play.

You've reached the final table

Congratulations!

Reaching the final table usually means you are in the top tier of the prize money so you can relax a bit. Now your goal is to be the victor.

OK, now is the time to take stock a bit, breathe deeply and get ready for that final hurdle. But you've done good, girl! Give yourself a pat on the back.

Chip stacks

First things first. Assess the chip situation at the table to see what you are up against. If there are a couple of short-stacked players at the table these guys are playing purely for survival. If they raise and you have a semi-decent hand, it is worth a call if you have enough chips to survive. Make sure, however, that there is no possibility for someone else to re-raise you so that you have to fold.

Hand requirements

You have probably been playing nine- or ten-handed throughout the tournament. The final table is where your short-handed game will come into play. As players get knocked out, the requirements for a decent starting hand are reduced. Hands such as A 7 become raising hands. You cannot wait around for the monster hands anymore, there is simply no time to waste.

Opposites attract

Tables take on a personality of their own. Try to play the opposite of the table. If it is very passive, use some aggression. If everyone is going mad with their all-ins, sit back and watch them knock each other out as you move up the money ladder without any effort.

Play the player...not the cards

Cards become less important as the final table progresses towards the end. The people are what matter now, and your judgement of them. Work out who you can steal pots from and who you can trap. This is difficult against the short stacks. If you are a big chip leader it is important to eliminate players fairly quickly before the blinds increase and put pressure on your own stack. However, there is no need to be reckless. Avoid getting into massive confrontations with bigger stacks as you will be the one who is eliminated.

Final table strategy

* Keep an eye on the short stacks and try to eliminate them if you sense them moving in with a weak hand.
* Don't let your stack become too low or else you will be vulnerable to others.
* If the table is playing tight take advantage and steal those blinds and vice versa.
* As players get eliminated, widen your selection of starting hands.

Heads-up strategy
Alone at last

Heads-up isn't a romantic interlude with someone you fancy, but one of the most rarified situations in the game of poker. Here, two players go head-to-head, usually at the culmination of a tournament.

Unfortunately, since most of us do not get to the latter stages of a tournament on a regular basis, we have very little opportunity to practise for it. Playing at home with your flatmate to see who does the dishes is not preparation nor the same as playing the final stages of a major tournament and claiming the spoils of victory.

This lack of practice and the inability of most of us to reach final tables accounts for the fact that it is always the same old faces who win tournaments – those who have been there before, had the practice and faced the pressure.

Make it just the two of us
The best advice for those playing for the first time is to ignore the crowd. You've already played well enough to reach this exalted position so there is no need to feel apprehensive, and no need to change your game style – well not too much!

A silk purse out of an A 2
As your opponents drop like flies, the number of starting hands you select to play gradually increases. For example, A 2 off-suit in a six- or nine-player game is a terrible hand and should be folded even if you are chip leader. However, in a heads-up match that same A 2 is a monster. Equally, K 8 is a hand that you should not play in a large field but in a heads-up situation, this can be very strong.

Rock or maniac?

Assuming that you both have the same number of chips when you begin the heads-up, how will you determine your game pattern choice? Will you be a rock or a maniac?

Remember that in a heads-up situation you are posting blinds every hand. If you are playing the rock you will check or fold to any bet and wait until you hit the hand you feel is strong enough to play. The advantage of this strategy is that your chances of losing in a hurry are slim and you may catch your opponent.

Crazy woman

Maniac, the other style choice in this situation, is quite lucrative and playing aggressively will help you steal most blinds from the rock and thus consolidate your position. Be aware that all this risk can be wiped out in one hand if the rock catches a hand and traps you.

After a few heads-up matches you will find that a balance of the two styles is perhaps the best way to play and most financially rewarding.

Top tips for the heads-up

* Widen your selection of starting hands.
* Keep an eye on chip stacks and blinds.
* Mix up your game a bit.
* Remember that position is very important.

You and your opponent

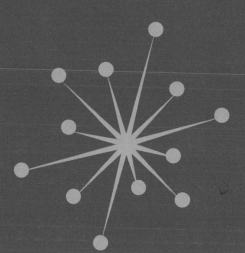

Projecting a strong front
Image is everything

One of the most important aspects of live play is your table image and presenting a strong image is vital to success.

Remember you're a woman!

People are very judgemental and poker players are no different. Working against you is the fact that you are a woman and some men will perceive you as easy money. Those less judgemental will form an opinion of you within a few hands of play.

Now, by table image I don't mean wearing excessive make-up or a cleavage-revealing dress, although both have been used effectively. You need to prey on their prejudices and preconceptions of women poker players and use this to your advantage.

Use the prejudice

Men who indulge the idea of women as an easy target at the poker table often find this prejudice returns to bite them on the backside. Use your skill and savvy to outplay them, and at the same time assess all the players to determine who is strong and who is weak. Make a mental note on each player's qualities and use it to aid your game. Target the weak and avoid the strong until the latter stages of a match.

The main misconception of female poker players is that women can't bluff! Who are they trying to kid. Use this to your utmost advantage!

Establishing a table image

* Make a stand – if someone is stealing your blinds show that you are not an easy target.
* The first time you are raised, re-raise even if you have nothing in your hand.
* Play strongly each hand you decide to play to indicate that you won't be messed with!
* Fool your opponents into thinking you a loose player by taking a hand to showdown with very weak holdings. The opposite is true if you are trying to establish a rock-like image.
* If bluffing, don't fold at the first sign of a raise – they could be out-bluffing you. Why not try a call or a re-raise.
* Playing the 'I'm a girl and I don't really know the rules' ploy can backfire but it might buy you some time while you get the feel for the table.

Chip tricks or cheap trick!

You've probably seen professionals on TV perform those clever chip tricks such as 'riffling' – while it may look really cool it actually achieves something much more important. On a subliminal level it implies that you have been on the poker scene for a while and playing live is not a new experience for you. This small signal may stop you getting bullied, so get riffling!

Types of player
Recognize your rock from your blender

Study the opposition. This mantra should be on your mind every time you sit down. Build up a mental picture of each one by observing the way they play and act around the table. Most girls do this anyway, so just sharpen up those natural-born skills.

Ask yourself this

* How many hands does he play?
* How often does he raise?
* What sort of hands is he showing at showdown after a raise?
* What sort of mood is he in?
* Are there any patterns to his play?
* Is he aggressive or passive?

Broadly speaking, players fall into four main types. Although crude portraits, these profiles will help you decide how to play your hand or when to make a marginal call.

The rock

This player will not call or raise unless he has a strong hand. He plays very few hands, seldom takes risks and rarely becomes involved. When he does show flickers of interest make sure you have a solid hand to catch him and bring him down. This player is the best to bluff against and he would rather pass than gamble.

The calling station

This opponent is very loose with her chips, renowned for calling any bet you throw at her regardless of what she holds. Her strategy is to call and get lucky on the flop to outdraw you. Don't bluff this player, as more often than not you will lose your chips. Play only your strong hands against her.

The maniac

This is the kind of player who is always forcing the action at the table. She raises, re-raises and will very often push all her chips into the pot with absolutely nothing since she has no fear and can sense weakness at the table. She plays like this to advertise her loose style so that when she picks up a monster she can be sure of success. It is a very high-risk strategy and unless you have a solid hand and can commit your entire stack, it is best not to get involved. You can lower your starting hand requirements with this player but remember, even maniacs got good cards!

The blender

The best players fall into this category. The blender tends not to play many hands and therefore builds up a little respect at the table. She gets involved at the right time on drawing hands, starts to bet more strongly and takes risks that the pot odds allow. She is more than capable of laying traps. She changes gear during the game at regular intervals and morphs into the other types of player to fool you and make you play against your usual pattern. Try to emulate this player but beware when she is sitting at your table.

The poker tell
You're telling me!

A 'tell' in poker is any habit, behaviour or physical reaction that gives players information about another player's hand. Nervous tics, fidgets and repetitive movements can give the game away.

Bright eyes

Many players wear sunglasses and caps at the table, because they know that the eyes rarely lie. Be aware that players may stare at their hole cards if it's a good hand. A quick glance means they are likely to fold. Sometimes people ask openly about an opponent's hand knowing that people can rarely look someone straight in the eye while being dishonest.

Pretty face

Facial expressions are important in the art of deciphering a tell. Many players look downwards at the table to avoid giving off any information. Study faces for nervousness (weak hand) or confidence (strong hand). Some people develop nervous tics when under pressure, so look for patterns.

Opposite reactions

A strong hand prompts a weak expression and vice versa. This usually applies to novice players but more experienced players may practise this as well. Players like to be actors – if they have a monster hand will look disinterested, saying 'is it my turn' or 'I guess I will play these cards'.

Cheer up!

Anxiety shows in people when they are confronted or anticipate confrontation. Physical changes occur including flexing of muscles, pupil dilation, raised heart beat and a dry throat. In poker, when someone has a big hand she is typically ready for confrontation and can exhibit some of these characteristics. You may see the chest expand abnormally, or notice the player's voice become slightly higher as she talks.

Bob the builder

The way a player stacks her chips can say a lot about the way she plays. Loose players tend to have sloppy and unorganized stacks while more conservative players keep well-organized, neat piles.

Hello Mr Chips!

A player who glances down at her chip stack after the flop, normally suggests that she has connected with it in some way. It may be subconscious but she might be planning her attack.

Memory lane

Some players sneak another look at their hole cards after the flop comes down to see if one of their cards is of the same suit. They would not do this if they had two suited cards already.

Groundhog day

The most revealing tell can be when a player habitually bets in certain situations. Maybe she always checks when she has the nuts.

Table etiquette

Mind your manners!

Breach of poker etiquette could be as embarrassing as breaking a heel at a wedding. At any table there is a collective understanding of what's right and wrong – but it's not complicated. Table etiquette is like good manners – simple courtesy and common sense will take you a long way. Here are a few things you should know.

Moodying = discussing your hand with an opponent to influence play

If you were playing a tournament, this would be a big taboo and would draw penalties from the tournament director. Some people try to discuss their hand to gauge a reaction from an opponent. By doing this they can determine the strength of their hand or goad the other player into making a certain play. For instance: 'I doubt I can do anything with this hand.'

Rub down = to berate another player when their inexperience has cost you

If, during a round of betting, another player makes a weak call and then proceeds to make a straight on the river, you may feel cross. More experienced players would have folded and you feel that you've been cheated out of some cash. But remember that you are a victim of luck and poker has a karmic side. What goes around comes around and the inexperienced player will soon learn that folding on an outside draw is usually more profitable. Chastising a novice player is simply bad manners and wouldn't be acceptable at a tournament or even a friendly girls' poker night.

Lack attention = raising, folding or calling out of turn

This is another sure-fire way to draw the wrath of your fellow gamblers. Simply watch the hand unfold in silence and enjoy the drama. The same goes for listening to your MP3 player or talking on your mobile phone. Try not to do it. Rude!

Splashing the pot = throwing your chips into the pot aggressively

Some people like to emulate the gambling they've seen in movies and toss their bet into the middle in a display of bravado. Retaining your feminine cool will reap all sorts of rewards in poker, so there is no need to sink to this level. If you 'splash your chips' it will be difficult to know the amount of your bet from the pot already in the centre. It is best to announce your bet or raise and simply slide or place the chips past the betting line.

Dealing etiquette = knowing who does what

The dealer, who has a white disk in front of her, passes the deck to the left to be shuffled, who then passes it to the dealer's right to be cut, and then it is returned to the dealer who will deal the cards clockwise. After each hand the dealer button shifts one position clockwise.

Winning gracefully
Don't be a sore loser or a crowing winner!

We women have many virtues denied to men and one of them is knowing how to both win and lose gracefully. When was the last time you saw two women resort to a punch-up because of a disagreement? Male testosterone sometimes gets in the way of good manners, even in the poker room.

No free-for-alls

This does not mean that you will have a ringside seat to a punch-up, as fighting in casinos is extremely rare and the security – with all that money flying around – is impeccable. People who fight in a casino are almost always banned from the establishment. What is not banned is verbal abuse, although even this is rare.

Sitting in the sin bin

Recently, the World Series of Poker introduced what is called the F-bomb rule which places people in a 'sin bin' for using profanities at the table. Players are compelled to stay away from the table for 10–15 minutes and play continues without them; their blinds are posted as if they were still playing. After a few punitive penalties like this everyone soon learns to keep their temper in check and their toilet tongue in their mouth.

If you make a lucky unorthodox call

Say you call a player's massive raise when only one or two cards in the deck can help you and you get lucky, be sure to apologize to your unfortunate opponent rather than jump out of your seat and punch the air with delight at your own good fortune!

If you are the recipient of a bad beat

Resist the urge to rant and rave at the 'idiot' who made the call. Tapping the table with your hand is a common way of saying 'nice hand'.

If you manage to win a lot of money in a short time

To 'win and run' is never appreciated. In this situation announce you will be leaving after a certain number of hands to give them the opportunity to win their money back.

Avoid being the 'table captain'

No one likes an 'I told you so' – someone who comments on every hand and tells everyone how they 'should' have played it.

Don't swear. It is not ladylike and could well get you banned from the table.

Coping with tilt
Life is a rollercoaster

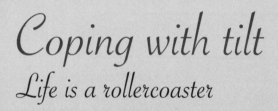

Poker is a game of luck and skill, and playing it can sometimes feel like riding a rollercoaster. When things don't go your way it creates feelings of unfairness and sometimes rage. When you lose control of these emotions and begin playing badly, this is called tilt.

Swings in your bankroll are as common to poker as dealing the cards and they must be accepted. Coping with fluctuations is a vital part of the game and in order to avoid the dreaded tilt here are a few simple guidelines.

Should I play? Am I on tilt?

* Am I fit to play?
* Am I in a good mood?
* Have I been drinking too much?
* Do I have personal issues with anyone at the table that will affect my play?
* Do I have the bankroll to sit down at this game?
* Is the game bigger than I am used to?
* Am I playing hands incorrectly due to a bad beat previously against me in the game and making bad decisions?

Self-control

Women tend to be good at keeping things together. However, the problem with going on tilt is that it is the actions of others that drives you wild and therefore is completely out of your control.

The causes of tilt

* Rude and aggressive opponents.
* People raising your blind every round.
* Other people's bad personal hygiene.
* People who berate your play without just cause.
* Getting outdrawn consistently and so on....

The best remedy is to take stock. If a player is rude or offensive simply ask her to stop or call a floor manager who will warn her and if necessary eject her from the game. If you are consistently outdrawn, reassess your moves and see what you could do to prevent it.

Take a breather

No matter what the cause the only one who will suffer in the end is you, so address and rectify the situation as soon as it occurs. Before you become really stressed walk away from the table for five minutes to calm yourself down and regroup – the worst thing that could happen is you may miss a blind or two.

It goes without saying that another weapon in your poker armoury is spotting tilt in others. Even the best players can suffer and therefore you can exploit this weakness in their game.

Gender advantage
Brain storm

We all know that there are big differences between male and female brains. What we need to look at is how that difference can be turned to our advantage when playing poker!

The brain is a complex subject but understanding where female strengths lie will go a long way at the poker table. Scientists have shown that there are differences, large and small. The subtle differences are the ways that we process language, information, emotion and cognition. Men and women differ in the way they process and estimate time, judge speed, do mental arithmetic and visualize three-dimensional objects. This may account for the fact that some professions are more male-dominated (pilots, mathematicians, mechanical engineers, architects and race car drivers).

Female advantage

Our brains are supposed to more driven by empathy and are geared towards identifying another's emotions and thoughts, while the male brain is more systematic, driven to explore the rules of how something works and the possible outcomes. Both qualities are incredibly useful in poker depending on how you use them.

Reading opponents is a large part of the game and this is where women have the edge. Women are more sensitive to fleeting facial expressions and are better at decoding non-verbal communication, picking up subtle nuances from tone of voice or facial expression – excellent qualities for poker!

Superior visuals

Females tend to show superior visual memory – especially for faces and names, and to have a longer attention span. This is great for poker as it allows you to build up a mental file on someone. Long attention spans are good for those long sessions at the table as well!

The evidence for female empathy has been studied in a variety of everyday situations. When it comes to sharing something like a games console it was found that the boys monopolized it and pushed the girls out of the way. This is mirrored at the poker table by men over-raising the pot and being bullies so their female opponents can't get a look in.

A punch vs bitchy remarks

Aggression is a big part of poker. In life men tend to show far more 'direct' aggression such as pushing and punching. Women tend to be more 'indirect' with their aggression, using gossip, exclusion and bitchy remarks.

By understanding these fundamental differences between the sexes, we girls can use the qualities we possess to our utmost advantage and turn male advantages into weak spots by preying on them!

Female intuition
Your secret weapon

Female intuition is one of those things that men deny exists. Women have that uncanny ability to look at the facts, apply their intelligence and judgement and say 'call it female intuition but I think we have gone wrong here!' And surprise, surprise, we are often right.

Fantastic secret weapon

Intuition is a mysterious sixth sense that women seem to possess; and it is a fantastic quality for the poker table. In fact, all human beings possess this intuitive ability, it is just that our brains accommodate its use more happily. We tend to think laterally, gathering information from all sorts of sources, and do not scorn emotional content in the mix. Men, on the other hand, think in a linear fashion, and are usually thought to be more logical and rational than women. We are supposed to lack the ability to reason logically.

This is not true, of course, but we are able to 'feel' our way through problems rather than solely look at the facts. We subconsciously pick up on the 'little things' and together with the facts we arrive at our conclusion.

Trust your instincts

At the poker table, we can employ this fantastic weapon when we are 'reading' other players' hole cards. Always be aware of your gut feeling. Be receptive to everything around you and factor all of this information into your decision, whether it is to fold, call or raise.

Are you being bluffed?

If you have an inkling that you are being bluffed, then you are probably right, but try to go through the reasoning behind your thought processes. Has he made that move before on you? Is there something in the way he is acting that makes you think this or is this decision totally based on instinct. If your heart is fighting what your brain is saying, I recommend listening to your heart – it will make you a far better player as your decisions have gone beyond the mathematical approach and have reached another level. Play the player not your cards!

Act, don't think

Don't think too much about this or your thoughts will become muddled. If your first instinct was to fold but instead you think and think, then call, more often than not you will probably be wrong. Follow your heart!

I am not saying ignore the mathematics of the game – of course it is an important and fundamental part of poker but there is a lot more than numbers, which makes the game fascinating and fun to play.

Flirting
The undisguised weapon

In poker it is essential to use absolutely every weapon at your disposal and flirting is a tremendous weapon. And so much fun! Do not be afraid – anything that gives you an edge is worth a try. The only proviso here is that if you don't feel comfortable flirting, don't do it.

All is fair in love and war

Poker is like warfare – everyone is an enemy and you choose how you want to attack them. Make the most of being a woman at the table, and use your minority status to your advantage – employ those feminine attributes to the max!

Give them the (eye) lash

Pick your target. If one of your male opponents keeps making references to the fact you are a woman, bat your eyelashes at him and smile sweetly; make him feel like he is the most important person at the table and then ... bring him down. It is all about lulling him into a false sense of insecurity.

Is your radar picking up warm, non-poker interest from one of the male players? Is he looking like he would prefer to socialize with you away from the poker table? Be aware that these men are really easy to play against because they don't want to ruin their chances by taking your chips off you.

Sweet-talking

You can use your sexuality to talk a man into folding, if you are careful and subtle enough. By making a 'you really shouldn't be calling me as I have a strong hand, sweetheart' type of reference, you may force him into folding for fear of looking stupid if he calls.

Dress the part

Dress for confidence and for yourself. If you are looking good, it will bolster your psychological armoury. Put some thought into what you wear to a poker game. Obviously, you don't want to look like a tart, but a well-chosen low-cut top is sure to divert a little attention away from the cards. A subtle spray of perfume can confuse the senses and a bit of make-up can enhance your appearance especially with the great low-level lighting that is normal in card rooms.

Be careful with the dumb blonde trick

If you are new to a game sometimes the 'dumb blonde' technique can work wonders. If you keep asking questions such as 'is it my turn?' or 'how much can I raise?' it is bound to put a couple of them on tilt in sheer frustration at having to answer. But the downside of this strategy is that they may treat you with distain. Employ carefully!

Nuts-holding strategies

When you are holding the nuts use some female-only diversionary tactics such as applying make-up while the river is dealt – it gives you an air of complete disinterest in the hand. When your opponent reads this as weakness and puts in a massive bet, you can then take him to the cleaners.

Girl power!

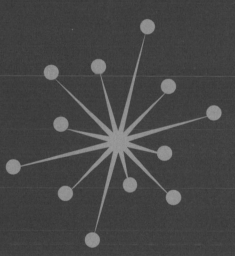

Female pros
Acknowledging the greats!

Women are steadily making a mark on the world poker scene. There are now ladies' poker tours and ladies-only events, which are great for the game. Although a woman has never won the main event at the WSOP there have been a number of great achievements.

Kathy Liebert

Kathy was the first woman ever to win a poker tournament with a buy-in of over $5,000 when she won the first Partypoker.com Million in 2002. She also won the televised 'Battle of the Sexes' where she beat 11 other men and women winning $100,000. She won a WSOP Bracelet in 2004 in the $1,500 Hold'em Shootout Event.

Before poker she worked in the corporate world as a business analyst and then in the stock market. Within a week of starting in tournament poker she had won $34,000 and launched her tournament career. She has been ranked in the top 20 players by *Card Player* magazine.

Annie Duke

Brought up in Concord, New Hampshire in a card-playing family, Annie majored in English and Psychology at Columbia University then enrolled as a graduate student in cognitive psychology at the University of Pennsylvania. After marrying her old friend Ben Duke she left academia behind and began to play in local poker rooms to pay the mortgage.

Her brother Howard Lederer is a well-known successful player, and he encouraged her to enter the WSOP in 1994. She ended up placing 13th after knocking her brother out! She then made the move to Las Vegas to play professionally.

In 2004 she beat 234 players in the $2,000 Omaha Hi/Lo Split WSOP event, winning her first bracelet. In the same year she won $2 million in the No Limit Hold'em Winner Takes All Tournament of Champions.

Jennifer Harman

Jennifer learned to play poker when she was eight years old as she watched her father play in a regular home game. When she was 21 Jennifer took up the game full time and specialized in No Limit Hold'em. She now plays in one of the biggest cash games in the world, the $4,000/$8,000 mixed game at the Bellagio in Las Vegas and is considered to be one of the best players around. Even though she mainly plays cash games she has won two WSOP Bracelets.

She lives in Las Vegas with her poker professional husband Marco Traniello. After receiving a kidney transplant she founded the organization CODA – Creating Organ Donation Awareness.

Barbara Enright

In 1986, Barbara won her first bracelet in the Ladies Championship. She won two more in 1994 and 1996. In 2005 she became editor-in-chief of *Woman Poker Player*, the first women's poker magazine.

Cyndy Violette

Cyndy was born in Queens, New York and her family relocated to Las Vegas when she was just 12 years old where she learned to play poker. She went professional after winning a Golden Nugget tournament in Seven-card Stud for $74,000, the most money to be won by a woman at that time. She received a lot of press and publicity and was featured in a *Playboy* article. In 2004 Cyndy won the Seven-card Stud high-low tournament at the WSOP. In the 2005 WSOP she made three final tables.

Jennifer Tilly

Jennifer is an actress turned poker player. She was nominated for an Academy Award for Best Supporting Actress for her role in Woody Allen's *Bullets over Broadway* (1994).

In 2005, she won the Ladies No Limit Hold'em event at the WSOP winning a bracelet and $158,625 beating 600 other players. She also won the third World Poker Tour Ladies Invitational Tournament held at the Bicycle Casino in Los Angeles in the same year.

Linda Johnson

Linda is sometimes referred to as the 'First Lady of Poker'. After finishing high school she went to work at the post office while attending college. When she turned 21 she started visiting Las Vegas and playing blackjack. Her father told her that if she wanted to gamble she should play poker as it was the one game that was truly beatable.

She found that she had a special ability for the game and played every available moment. Linda entered the WSOP Ladies Seven-card Stud Tournament in 1980, deciding in advance that if she performed well, she would quit her job at the post office and move to Las Vegas to become a professional poker player. She finished fifth and embarked on a new career.

In 1992 she bought *Card Player Magazine* along with friends Denny Axel and Scott Rogers. They turned the black-and-white newsprint publication into a full-colour glossy magazine to great success.

During her time as a publisher until 2000, Linda was instrumental in helping to establish many other poker projects including the World Poker Industry Conference, the World Poker Players Conference and the Tournament Directors Association. After she left publishing, she ventured into the highly successful card player cruises. Among her clients were the Partypoker.com Million Cruise. She won a bracelet in the WSOP 1997 and has had much success on the tournament circuit.

Victoria Coren

Victoria is a well-known television presenter, newspaper columnist and author in the UK. She presents television poker shows and writes a weekly poker column for the *Guardian* newspaper. Her biggest win to date is the European Poker Tour (EPT) London Event in 2006, taking £500,000. She was the first woman to win an EPT event in the three years it has been running. She was also the winner of the UK 2004 Celebrity Poker Challenge.

Top women pros give advice to beginners

Tales from the felt

A selection of top female players give us their insight into the game and share their experiences in the world of poker.

Lucy 'Golden Ovaries' Rokach

Lucy Rokach from the UK managed to get three first-place finishes at the Victoria Casino in London in the same year as well as two firsts in Dublin. Before she fell into poker by accident she sold cars for a living. She met her partner, Tom Gibson, over the poker table. She describes her poker game as a 'high wire act'!

She is all for positive discrimination at the poker table and welcomes ladies-only events. She has found over the years that men at the poker table do not like assertive women. She feels that men believe that they have a monopoly on risk-taking and this comes across at the poker table.

One time she was just starting out she came across 'a foul-mouthed little man who couldn't tolerate me winning and would always chase me down. So when I realised the situation, I made sure I always had the nuts against him whilst at the same time he could see me persistently bluffing others. I drove him crazy, to the detriment of his bankroll!'

Lucy's advice to a beginner is 'Don't be intimidated!'

Isabelle 'No Mercy' Mercier

Isabelle is in her early thirties and is Canadian. Her most notable achievement was winning the World Poker Tour Ladies Night II. She also came fifth in the WSOP $5,000 No Limit Hold'em in 2006.

She was three years old when she discovered poker playing with her father her uncles. She was a lawyer before she started working in the poker world as poker manager of the Aviation Club de France in Paris. She feels that poker has given her the freedom she has always looked for. Isabelle describes her game as 'Intelligent-Aggressive'.

Isabelle thinks that female-only events are great for poker as they bring more women into the game. Once they do that they start asking for more and enter the mixed tournaments. She feels that men tend to treat women as conservative players but points out that most amateur men are exactly the same! Every time she plays with men who don't know who she is, they give her a lot of credit, so she gets away with a lot because they see her as a conservative player!

She advises the beginner to start online to get a feel for the game and the rules. Her mother plays a $1 Sit 'n Go everyday and is becoming really good!

Katja Thater

Katja is from Germany where it is still not legal to publish tournament winnings in detail. She has made many final tables and placed twice in the money in WSOP events in 2006. She played for the German team in the Poker Nations Cup in 2006.

She discovered poker in 1999 at the European Championship in Baden, Austria after replacing her husband at a table during a bathroom break in a high-limit cash game. When she won her very first pot she was hooked. She still trains horses but has quit her job as a director of an event and marketing company in Germany. She loves the fact she is now her own boss as she is playing poker.

Katja describes her poker game as 'tight-aggressive and very patient'.

She advises female beginners 'not to be afraid of your male opponents. The enemy is not sitting in front of you it is sitting in your own head'.

Loose ends

Hosting a home game
Your place or mine?

When you are confident enough in the basics of the game, why not invite a few friends around for something to eat, a few drinks and a game of poker...and impress them with your new-found skills.

What kind of game should we play?

First things first; you need to decide what kind of poker you are going to play. Do you want to hold a tournament-style evening or purely a cash game? What stakes do you want to play? How long do you want to play? If you are putting on a tournament, is it a freeze-out or a re-buy?

Establish a starting time and make a blind structure. Use the chart below for guidance – it has 15-minute blinds with a 2,000 starting stack.

Sample blind structure

Blinds	Time
25–50	15 mins
50–100	15 mins
75–150	15 mins
100–200	15 mins
150–300	15 mins
200–400	15 mins

Re-buys?

If you plan to have re-buys it is normal for the tournament to become a freeze-out after the third level. It is also possible to offer an add-on to boost the pot. Once the freeze-out stage has been reached, decide on a payout structure. If there are ten people playing it is normal for the top three spots to share the pot 50–30–20 per cent. Put your most punctual friend in charge of the stop watch, then shuffle up and deal!

You will need

Poker table or round table with a felt cloth
Comfortable chairs
Several decks of cards
Set of chips (with 3 or 4 denominations)
Dealer button
Clock or stopwatch
Food and drink

Munchies

It is always a good idea to have some poker-friendly snacks lying around. Avoid foods that are messy or greasy as this will rub off on the cards. Encourage your guests to keep their drinks off the table and have a smoking policy that suits everyone. You might like to lay on some sort of entertainment for those who crash out of the tournament early.

Playing online poker
Find a game – choose a name

For all you new girls out there, cyberspace is an excellent place to practise your new passion. For complete poker virgins the process of playing online is outlined below and is really as easy as clicking a mouse.

Site-search

1 Decide which site you would like to play on. There are a myriad of them out there of all shapes and sizes. The bigger ones may reassure you psychologically in terms of security of your money or credit card details, but rest assured, this industry is very well policed. Find a site and download its software.

2 Take a few seconds to familiarize yourself with the site – most online poker sites look almost identical. After a good look around, find the button that says log-in – if this is not obvious look for it under the 'lobby' banner. You need to register as a new user. The only details required at present are your name, address and contact details. You will need to think of a clever alias by which the cyber world will know you. No one but the registering company will have your personal details and your anonymity is guaranteed.

3 Now look for the 'play' or 'fun' money area. Once you click on this you will see a list of games that are arranged by game type, starting time, number of players etc. Again, take a few minutes to familiarize yourself with this and choose the game that suits you best by clicking on it.

4 You will be sent to a 'table' and will be seated automatically. Once all the places are filled the tournament will begin. The advantage of playing online is that the computer will handle the cards, chips and dealer button so you can focus on your game. If you feel like being social there is a chat box to talk to people – they might be in Japan, America or Australia. Most people use this facility and it is quite fun.

5 When you are ready for some real money play, hit the button marked cashier and make a deposit. You can be assured that your transaction and card details are secure – these are billion-dollar companies – and they employ the latest technology to safeguard your credit card and the personal details you give.

6 Playing online is a great source of fun and good practice. Always stay within a comfortable buy-in level so that the game remains enjoyable. The benefits of playing online are that it is done from the comfort of your home and there is a game whenever you want one.

Learn the language of cyberspace

Here is a list of the most commonly used online phrases.

TY	thank you
WP	well played
UL	unlucky
NH	nice hand
GG	good game
PP	pocket pair
NB	nice bet
BB	bad beat
LOL	laugh out loud
STT	Single table tournament
MTT	Multi-table tournament
Free-rolls	Free to enter tournaments
Cash games	To suit all budgets

Bankroll management and tracking results

Cash is king (or queen)

As a poker journalist I have been lucky enough to meet the great and the good in the poker world – and a few impostors along the way. To a man (and woman) most players monitor their results to see how they are doing and to check whether their bank balances are up or down. It is also a great way to check where you have better success and where you consistently lose.

Drawing up a spreadsheet and noting the following every time you play is one way to go.

Bankroll chart

Date:

Event:

Casino/online:

Tournament or cash game:

Number of entrants:

Buy-in:

Re-buy/top-up:

Placing:

Winnings:

Random Notes:

(for example, bad call, unlucky river, shouldn't have called with the xxx...)

Bankroll balance:

There are more sophisticated charts that you could create but these details are the minimal basics. You can be sure that the professionals keep much more detailed accounts, including hands played and notes on their opponents.

Record slackers

Now I can't overemphasize the importance of keeping records and I can't tell you how many people who do not keep an accurate account are deluding themselves.

Unfortunately, I have to count myself in this number until I started keeping track. I was sure I was ahead of the game because I could quite easily recall winning $500 here and $1,000 there. It wasn't until I began to make a list that I realized I had entered 10–20 tourneys before winning. Ten tourneys at $50 each soon adds up and when you lose $50 it is easily forgotten. However, winning $500 is remembered for a long time!

However, it is always fun recording that big win but have the self-discipline to record those losses. There is a lot of satisfaction to be gained from keeping up-to-date charts.

Keep your bankroll separate

It is always a good idea to keep your bankroll separate from your day-to-day spending. You don't want to find you've lost the gas bill money in a disastrous cash game at the casino. If playing online, try to keep a separate credit card just for this so it doesn't get out of control.

Don't allow things to get out of hand

Always play within your means. Never put all your eggs in one basket by investing the whole lot in one tournament. Ideally, you should never stake more than 5 per cent of your bankroll in any one session. There are inevitable swings in poker and sometimes they aren't in your favour. To know how much to sit down with in cash games is personal choice but it is normal to have 300 times the big blind. So, if you are playing in a $1–$2 game, then $600 would be sufficient. Of course, you could sit down with the minimum, but you would have to hope to get lucky with the first pot you entered.

Cheating and collusion
Bad guys are rare but there

Where there is money involved, there will be people willing to cheat to profit themselves. But you can take some comfort from the fact that anyone engaged in such activity will probably not bother to do so at the small stakes beginners' tables. Anyone with a good scam would surely perpetrate it where the risk is worth the reward.

Ten pairs of beady eyes

At most tables there are nine other people besides yourself playing – that means many extra, more experienced, eyes than yours being vigilant. Also, once you get to the money stage of almost every tournament, the casino or card-room will provide a professional dealer to deal the final table, and this person will be experienced at noticing anything amiss.

I have been playing cards for years in every type of casino and card-room and am happy to say that I have never come across any form of cheating that I was aware of. Anyone caught cheating is not only banned, but as casinos have reciprocal agreements, they also run the risk of being banned from every casino in the country.

Collusion

More difficult to spot is collusion. This is also plain and simple cheating – just in a different way. Collusion is when two or more players collude or scheme to extract money or chips from other players. In a tournament situation you will have other people there who will be vigilant and watching for this. Also the rules dictate that at showdown each player must show their hands face up to all in order to claim the pot.

In a form of collusion known as 'chip dumping', one player deliberately passes his chips on to a 'partner' to place them in a stronger chip position. As stated earlier you have the right to ask to see every hand – even if the player wants to muck – especially if you feel this is happening. Being aware and asserting your rights will help you not be a victim of these cheats.

Don't be afraid to complain

If you feel you have noticed something untoward, a quiet word in the floor manager's or tournament director's ear will ensure she monitors the situation. Also, if you are not entirely satisfied with the result of your complaint you always have the option of never returning to that establishment again.

Only English spoken here

In the United States and in the United Kingdom the language of the table is English and must be used at all times. If another language is being spoken and you suspect that it is giving the speakers an edge you must bring it to the floor manager's attention immediately.

Cheating online
Suspect play in cyberspace

While cheating and collusion in live tournaments is very rare, sadly, the same cannot be said about the online game.

Online watchdogs

As an online player, you have the protection, might and force of billion-dollar corporations behind you and they are very vigilant in stamping out every form of collusion in order to safeguard themselves and their customers. The lengths taken by major Internet-based poker rooms to ensure there is no collusion is vast. Online tracking systems:

* Monitor each player's account for unusual activity.
* Monitor if two players are always logged on to the same table.
* Monitor the hands, bets and folds of each player on every table.
* Monitor the IP (internet provider) addresses of every player to ensure they are not on the same table/game. Sites only allow one IP address on any one table.
* Monitor money transactions between players for money laundering.

There are different forms of cheating and collusion you should look out for. With the advent of online messaging systems you have no way of knowing if two players are talking to each other and disclosing their hole cards, for example. This can also be done over the phone. If two players are from the same location, watch their play a little more carefully. Are they getting involved in big pots together or are they avoiding confrontation?

Big-time cheats

There are more sophisticated ways of cheating – a big player may have more than one computer and IP address in his residence. This way he can be seated at more than one seat at the table. This is known as self-collusion. Most cheaters are normally spotted by other players and reported so their hand histories can be checked. Sites are very proactive in following up these complaints.

There are more subtle ways of cheating online which may be hard to spot by a beginner. The good news is that it is not worth their while to frequent the tiny stakes. One trick is for two or more players to sit down at the same table and if somebody raises who is not part of their 'team' they begin re-raising amongst themselves making it impossible for the original raiser to continue with their betting. This is known as collusion.

Another way is far more common and is known as 'soft-playing'. If you are in a pot with your best friend or partner and you are unhappy about taking a lot of chips / money off them you might find yourself checking down the hand – be careful if you are the last to act after the river and you are holding the 'nuts', you may well find yourself accused of cheating.

Knowing the basic mathematics of poker

I've got your number!

Poker is not only a game of skill and luck, it is also a game of numbers. Being aware of the basics will go a long way to improving your game.

Know your odds

The best tournament players always know the odds of their hand winning an all-in confrontation against other hands and this can be a useful tool. Knowing your numbers can impress and the odd comment can create an air of superiority, which may enhance your table image.

Combinations

In No Limit Texas Hold'em there are 1,326 possible two-card combinations for a starting hand. This is reduced to 1,225 for your opponent to be holding after you have seen your hand. If you play a hand through there are 19,600 possible flops and a massive 2,118,760 full-board combinations. These numbers may sound scary but in practice just knowing vaguely what they might be significantly enhances your chance of success.

Chances

The chances of being dealt a pocket pair are 16/1. If you do get dealt a pair you have a 12 per cent chance that this will turn into three of a kind or trips on the flop. When you are not holding a pair, one of your cards will only connect on the flop about one third of the time and by the time the river is dealt this increases to 49 per cent.

On the draw
If you flop an open-ended straight draw it will complete 34 per cent of the time.

The flop will come...
The flop will be all one suit some 5 per cent of the time. It will be two-suited cards 55 per cent and the other 40 per cent of the time it will be a rainbow (one of each suit).

Hand match-ups pre-flop if there is an all-in

This table gives some examples of hand match-ups pre-flop if there was an all-in situation with no further betting. It is interesting to see which marginal hands are stronger against some of the premium hands.

Hands	Win %	Lose %	Draw %
A♣ A♦ vs K♣ K♠	81.5	18	0.5
A♣ A♦ vs Q♠ J♠	80	19.5	0.5
A♥ A♦ vs K♣ 10♥	86	13.5	0.5
A♣ K♣ vs A♠ 7♥	72.5	23	4.5
A♠ 6♦ vs A♠ 2♣	38	28	34
A♣ K♣ vs 2♥ 2♣	50	49.5	0.5
A♣ K♣ vs Q♠ Q♣	43.5	56	0.5
A♥ K♣ vs 8♥ 9♥	61	38.5	0.5
A♣ J♥ vs Q♣ 9♠	58.5	41	0.5
A♣ 6♠ vs 9♥ 10♥	51.5	48	0.5

Charts

Numbers, probabilities and lots of other stuff

The main chart is a reference guide to determine what your chances are of winning a hand after the flop has come down. 'Outs' refers to how many cards are theoretically left in the deck (47 cards) that could help you make your hand. For example, if you have a flush draw and an open ended straight draw you have 15 outs – you have a 31.9 per cent chance of making your hand. The more 'outs' you have the more you should call a bet. In contrast if you are waiting for a middle card to a straight – also known as a Gutshot – there are only four cards that could possibly help and therefore your chance of winning the hand is only 8.5 per cent .

The probability of your Aces winning against different numbers of players

Number of opponents	Odds of A A winning
1	85%
2	73%
3	64%
4	56%
5	49%
6	44%
7	39%
8	35%
9	31%

The probability that one or more of your opponents has a better Ace on a ten-seater table

Your hand	Other hands
A Q	8%
A J	15%
A 10	22%
A 9	28%
A 8	34%
A 7	39%
A 6	44%
A 5	49 %
A 4	53%
A 3	57%
A 2	61%

The odds of making your hand after the flop has come down

Outs	Draw	Turn (47 cards left)		River (46 cards left)		Turn and River	
		Odds	Per cent	Odds	Per cent	Odds	Per cent
20		1.35 : 1	42.6%	1.30 : 1	43.5%	0.48 : 1	67.5%
19		1.47 : 1	40.4%	1.42 : 1	41.3%	0.54 : 1	65%
18		1.61 : 1	38.3%	1.56 : 1	39.1%	0.60 : 1	62.4%
17		1.76 : 1	36.2%	1.71 : 1	37%	0.67 : 1	59.8%
16		1.94 : 1	34%	1.88 : 1	34.8%	0.75 : 1	57%
	Flush & Open-ended Straight Draw						
15		2.13 : 1	31.9%	2.07 : 1	32.6%	0.85 : 1	54.1%
14		2.36 : 1	29.8%	2.29 : 1	30.4%	0.95 : 1	51.2%
13		2.62 : 1	27.7%	2.54 : 1	28.3%	1.08 : 1	48.1%
	Flush & Gutshot Straight Draw						
12		2.92 : 1	25.5%	2.83 : 1	26.1%	1.22 : 1	45%
11		3.27 : 1	23.4%	3.18 : 1	23.9%	1.40 : 1	41.7%
10		3.70 : 1	21.3%	3.60 : 1	21.7%	1.60 : 1	38.4%
	Flush Draw						
9		4.22 : 1	19.2%	4.11 : 1	19.6%	1.86 : 1	35%
	Open-ended Straight Draw						
8		4.88 : 1	17%	4.75 : 1	17.4%	2.18 : 1	31.5%
7		5.71 : 1	14.9%	5.57 : 1	15.2%	2.59 : 1	27.8%
6		6.83 : 1	12.8%	6.67 : 1	13%	3.14 : 1	24.1%
5		8.40 : 1	10.6%	8.20 : 1	10.9%	3.91 : 1	20.4%
	Gutshot Straight Draw						
4		10.75 : 1	8.5%	10.50 : 1	8.7%	5.07 : 1	16.5%
3		14.67 : 1	6.4%	14.33 : 1	6.5%	7.01 : 1	12.5%
2		22.50 : 1	4.3%	22.00 : 1	4.4%	10.88 : 1	8.4%
1		46.00 : 1	2.1%	45.00 : 1	2.2%	22.50 : 1	4.3%

Frequently asked questions
What if?

In this section we address situations that may arise during a poker tournament. Rules vary from casino to card-room across the world so it is always best to check as they are by no means universal.

What happens if more than one person is knocked out in the same hand in a tournament?
If more than one player is eliminated in the same hand, the person with the largest chip stack at the start of the hand regardless of their hand will be awarded the highest place on the ladder.

What happens if a player arrives late for a tournament?
Players who have already bought into the tournament but have not arrived by the time the first hand is dealt will, at the tournament director's discretion, be assigned a seat and issued with chips. They will then be penalized for the blinds and antes they may have missed.

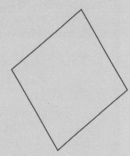

How do I know where I am sitting in a tournament?
Each table will seat a maximum of ten players with players evenly distributed between all tables. Seats will be randomly assigned by the tournament director.

As people get knocked out of the tournament how do players get moved around?
If the number of players differs by two or more between any two tables, the tables are balanced by moving a player from the larger table to the smaller table. It is normally the person who is about to post their Big Blind. They will be moved to the space on the next table in the fairest possible way relating to the blinds.

What is a dead button?

If the Big Blind busts out of the tournament and is not replaced by a player from another table, the button moves to the player who posted the Small Blind and the player to the left of the former Big Blind assumes the Big Blind. There is now no Small Blind for that hand. On the next deal, the button moves to the empty seat and the two players to the left post the normal blinds. This will result in the same player being the dealer two hands in a row.

When the Small Blind vacates the tournament and is not replaced by a player from another table, the button does not move. The player who was the Big Blind will now post the Small Blind and the player to his left will post the Big Blind. This will mean that the same player will be the dealer two hands in a row.

Who is the tournament director?

The tournament director is responsible for all table, seating and dealer decisions. He/she is responsible for the handling of the clock. In the case of disputes and rulings the tournament director will have final authority.

Who posts which blinds when it reaches the heads-up stage?

In heads-up play, the player on the button is the Small Blind and acts first before the flop and last after the flop. The first card is dealt to the non-dealer.

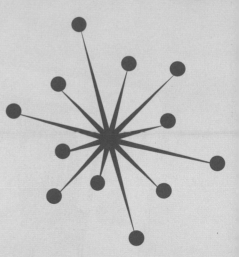

How is the pay-out structure worked out?
The prize-pool is the total number of buy-ins, re-buys and add-ons. If you are playing a ten-seater tournament the winner will receive 50 per cent, second place 30 per cent and third 20 per cent. In a multi-table tournament 10 per cent of the field should be paid with the winner receiving 40 per cent.

How much should I tip the dealer?
Sometimes you are not allowed to tip the dealer due to country laws but if you are, it is normal to tip around 5 per cent of your winnings.

What is an under-raise?
An under-raise occurs when a player raises a previous bet but has to go all-in. If his bet is less than double the original bet it is considered an under-raise. The betting is now stopped for that round and other players may only call.

What happens if a player takes a very long time to make a decision and the game is being slowed down?
Once a reasonable time has passed you may call the clock on a slow player via the tournament director. The player will then be given one minute to decide on his action. If he does not make a decision his hand will be declared dead.

What happens if somebody calls out of turn?
If somebody calls out of turn his bet will stand unless the pot is raised before the action reaches that player.

What is slow rolling?
Slow rolling is when you are holding the nuts and it has come to showdown and you take ages to declare your hand – it is considered very bad etiquette.

What is a sign-up bonus on online poker sites?
The sign-up bonus is an incentive that poker sites offer when you first deposit cash with them. They will give you an extra amount of money after you have complied with certain criteria such as a certain number of raked hands.

Game analysis

Case study 1
Playing suited connectors

Situation

You are playing in a $20 freeze-out tournament. You have managed to reach the halfway period and are dealt 8 ♥ 9 ♥. You are on the button and there has been one caller so far. The blinds are at 50/100 and you have 1,400 in front you. What should you do? Call, raise or fold?

Solution

Other than a big pair, one of the favourite hands of most pros is suited connectors, especially 8 9 or 9 10. There are so many ways in which your hand can improve with these cards and if played correctly you can win without actually hitting. Obviously the ways it can improve are through pairing up, a straight or a flush.

In the above situation you should raise perhaps 300, because as there is only one caller and he has only called and not raised, it is likely he has a marginal hand (say K ♣ 5 ♦). Although he is ahead at this point, he has a weak hand and the only real hope he has is to hit his King and even then he will be worried about his kicker (see Case Study 3 on page 158).

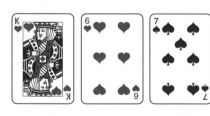

THE FLOP COMES DOWN

After the flop

Although he has hit his King, believe it or not, this is the ideal flop for YOU. You have hit your 8 and also have a straight draw and a flush draw. Therefore the outs that you have are: any Heart for the flush (nine cards), any of two remaining 5s or three remaining 10s for a straight, a remaining 8 (two cards), or a 9 (three cards) – therefore 20 outs with two cards to come.

A follow-up raise from you now will either cause him to fold (although he has a King he will be worried about his kicker), or he will build the pot, with the odds of winning in your favour.

FLOP - K ♥ 6 ♥ 7 ♠ – TURN CARD J ♦

The turn card does not benefit anyone and the situation remains the same. You should still raise in the hope of making your opponent fold or again build the pot.

FLOP K ♥ 6 ♥ 7 ♠ TURN CARD J ♦ RIVER CARD 5 ♣

The river

That 5 on the river is a miracle card for you, although now your opponent thinks it is a miracle card for him. As he now has two pairs, crucially with top pair (K K), you should be able to extract all his money. The beauty of playing suited connectors (or even connectors) is that your opponent does not see it coming. As the situation stands, the only hand he knows will beat him is trips (unlikely to be held) or K J, K 6 or K 7. Therefore, feeling so confident he will probably call or bet an all-in anticipating victory.

Note: If the river card had been the 5 ♥ it would still give your opponent the same hand but he would be wary of a flush and extracting all his chips would be difficult.

Case study 2
Pocket Aces late in tournament

Situation

You are in a tournament with an average stack in front you. It is a satellite tournament with the top four players winning a ticket into a bigger event. There are seven players left and it is almost bubble time. You look down at your cards and see a pair of Aces. The person sitting in first position goes all-in and so does position 2 and 3. Should you fold, call, or even raise to deter players behind you?

Position

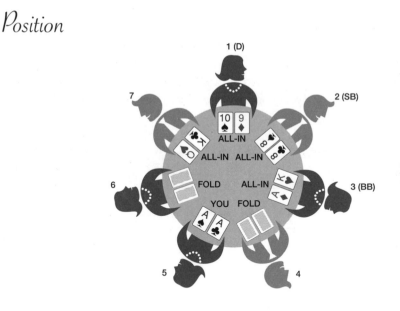

Player 1 All-in 10 ♠ 9 ♦
Player 2 All-in 8 ♣ 8 ♠
Player 3 All-in A ♦ K ♥
Player 4 Fold
Player 5 YOU A ♠ A ♣
Player 6 Fold
Player 7 All-in K ♣ Q ♥

Solution

This is one of the few situations in poker when you should lay down pocket Aces (fold). The thought process is that as long as there are two people all-in in front of you and others to decide, at least one or two are sure to be eliminated (except in the unlikely event of a split pot) and you should not risk being the one eliminated. Remember in the bubble you are waiting for the next player out. Granted, you are well ahead pre-flop and in most cases you could triple up, but in this case winning is not important, just finishing in the top four is what matters.

| FLOP | | | TURN | RIVER |

Lay down your Aces and let the others take each other out. As you can see, with so many callers the chances of you being outdrawn have increased and in the above scenario you would not only have lost to the straight but also the trip 8s. By sitting back you have seen three players eliminated although you may have had the best starting hand.

One other situation when you must lay down Aces, no matter how hard it seems, is when there are four or more people all-in in front of you. Although you are almost certainly ahead pre-flop, the chances of one of the other pairs pairing up is very strong and could eliminate you. Let the other four go at it and watch the three others get eliminated, moving you closer to the final table.

Case study 3
High card, weak kicker

Situation

You are sitting in the Big Blind with K ♦ 2 ♠. There is a medium raise from late position and the Small Blind has called the raise. Should you fold, call or raise?

Position

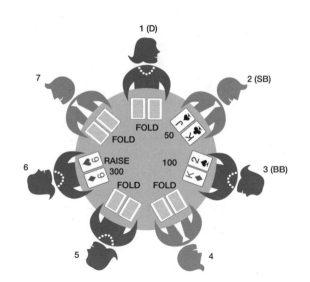

Player 1   Fold
Player 2   50 SB   K ♣ J ♠
Player 3   100 BB   K ♦ 2 ♠
Player 4   Fold
Player 5   Fold
Player 6   Raise 300   9 ♥ 9 ♦
Player 7   Fold

Solution

The hand you are holding is likely to be the worst hand in the pot. Even if you hit the King on the board, the likelihood is that you will be out-kicked. It is not worth making a re-raise as with this number of callers already in the pot someone is bound to call you.

The best thing to do in this situation is fold. Additionally, with two callers, one is bound to be trapping with a strong hand. A raise from you will precipitate a potential all-in or further raise, not something you want to be involved in with a K 2. You have to fold. Imagine a flop of A K 5.

After the flop

Now would you risk more chips betting no one is holding an Ace? Also, would you risk more chips betting no one has a King with a better kicker?

If the turn and river brought a 10 and a 2, you may falsely think you were very strong with two pairs but let's see how many hands could be beating you: A K, A 10, A 5, A 2, K 10, K 5, A A, K K, 10 10, 5 5 and 2 2. That is 11 hands beating you assuming you hit both cards. If you only hit the K you can add: A, A J, A 9, A 8, A 7, A 6, A 4, A 3, K Q, K J, K 9, K 8, K 7, K 6, K 4 and K 3.

Now can you see the importance of a strong kicker?

Case study 4
Nice pair, bad timing

Situation

In a multi-table tournament you are in first position on a ten-seater table and find yourself holding a pair of Jacks. What do you do?

Solution

Although a pair of Jacks is quite a strong hand it is marginalized by your position. Raise three or four times the Big Blind. This will eliminate all but the stronger hands and allow you to see the flop. The reason you don't go all-in is that anyone holding an A K or A Q or even K Q may be tempted to call and you could be in serious trouble, and facing elimination.

   If you raise as suggested your opponents will think you have a similar hand to theirs or a pair. If you do not see a higher face card after the flop, you can go all-in – chances are you can claim the pot. However, if there is a re-raise to your raise and one or two all-ins after that, you are sure to have several face cards (A, K, Q) and the chances of your Jacks holding up are very slim. Fold and wait for another opportunity.

SCENARIO 1 FLOP

If the above flop came up it would be easy to lay down your Jacks.

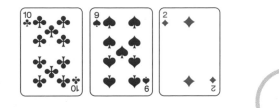

SCENARIO 2 FLOP

In the above scenario the only correct move is to now go all-in. This will deter those with a strong hand i.e A K, A Q from calling now as they only have 6 outs with two cards to come.

Note: The reason Jacks-in-the-hole are considered so tricky is that anyone playing pocket Queens would be playing the same way and would wait for the flop and see if there was an Ace or King for them. So going all-in now could draw out the pocket Queens and send you packing.

Case study 5

Nice pair, good timing

Situation

In a multi-table tournament you find yourself in first position on a ten-seater table holding a pair of Jacks. Blinds are 500–1,000 and you have flat-called the blind. Player 2 has raised $4,000 of his $15,000 stack and everyone has folded to you. What do you do?

Position

1 (D)

6

2 (SB)

J♠ J♣
1,000

K♣
A♥
4,000

5

3 (BB)

4

Player 1   J♠ J♣ 1,000
Player 2   A♠ K♣ 4,000
Player 3   Fold
Player 4   Fold
Player 5   Fold
Player 6   Fold

Solution

In this situation your timing could not be better. The good news is that **Player 2** has done all the hard work for you by eliminating everyone else. The likelihood is that he is holding A K, A Q, A J or a medium pair. In most cases the pair will be lower than yours. You should re-raise all-in.

The reason you go all-in rather than call is that with five cards to come, the chances of an Ace, King or Queen appearing on the board is strong and any higher face card on the flop should be your cue to a fast exit.

An all-in raise will leave him with two choices – call or fold. As he has already raised and shown strength, your re-raise implies you are very strong. If he is a good player he will most likely fold unless holding A A, K K or Q Q, which is extremely unlikely as the chance of two pairs being dealt in one round is extremely unlikely. A player holding A K may risk a call, and it is a risk, but with only six outs you are in a good situation to double up.

Case study 6
Tripling up?

Situation
You are holding 6 ♦ 6♥ in early position and have called a minimum raise pre-flop. How should you play them with these various flops?

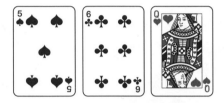

SCENARIO 1 FLOP

Solution
One of the strongest and most deceptive hands in poker is trips (three of a kind) and especially low-value trips. Higher trips are easier to spot as usually they are raised pre-flop. Often a player holding 2 2, 4 4, 6 6 or similar will not raise pre-flop and will wait to see what comes. Anyone hitting a Queen in the above situation will feel strong, especially if they have a strong kicker (Ace or King). A player holding Q 6 or Q 5 will feel indestructible and will she is slow-playing and trapping you, while you know you are about to take all her chips.

After the flop 1
If the above flop comes you should check and await a bet. Raising may scare everyone off or alert them to your strength. Just flat-call a raise and do not re-raise. Allow your opponents to catch a card and give them every chance to come at you. Even if they hit the Queen remember that another Queen may give them trips but will give you a full house. Always be aware that if a higher card hits the deck, someone else may have a pocket pair and therefore have a higher set than you.

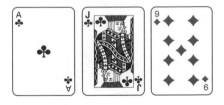

SCENARIO 2 FLOP

After the flop 2

If the flop, as above, shows all high cards you can fold and get away cheaply.

SCENARIO 3 FLOP

After the flop 3

A pair in the hole that hits is virtually unbeatable – except in the above scenario. Although normally you would want your opponent to hit her Ace and bet at you, here you should raise a very large amount to close out the hand and not trap, as anyone chasing and hitting the flush could damage your stack significantly.

All-in!

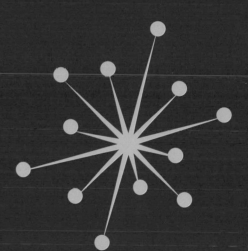

Common nicknames for poker hands

Name calling!

Though the origins of poker are unclear, what is apparent is that the game has been played since the early 19th century and was a favourite pastime of cowboys in the American Wild West. And while this is the source of many of the nicknames for hands, newer variants emerge from each new generation that discovers the game. Online or offline, they become universal and sometimes there's even a little story to go with them!

American Airlines This refers to holding a pair of Aces in the hole. They are also referred to as Bullets or Pocket Rockets.

Big Slick Holding a starting hand of Ace King. This hand is also amusingly referred to as the Anna Kournikova – looks good but never wins! Little Slick refers to Ace Queen in the hole.

Canine A dog of a hand! – A King 9 in the hole. Rarely wins as more often than not you will be out-kicked.

Computer Hand A Queen 7. From a story that a computer proved these were the most commonly occurring cards on the flop.

Cowboys When holding a monster pair of Kings in the hole.

Dead Man's Hand When you are holding Ace 8 and hit two pairs. This is the hand that was being played by legendary lawman and gambler Wild Bill Hickok when he was shot dead.

Ducks Holding a pair of 2s – also knows as deuces. When they make a set they are sometimes known as Huey, Dewey and Louie after Donald Duck's nephews.

Fish Hooks Holding a pair of Jacks.

Jackson Five Holding a Jack and a 5 in the hole – also known as Motown.

Kojak Holding a King and a Jack in the hole; named after the infamous detective.

Newlyweds A starting hand of King Queen.

Rags to Riches To be in the Big Blind with a hand you wouldn't normally call with, like 2 3 unsuited, but since you are in the Big Blind you check. When the flop falls Ace 4 5 your rags just became riches with the straight!

Roger A starting hand of 10 4, referring to a '10-4' response of 'Roger'.

Route 66 Pocket 6s.

Siegfried and Roy A popular nickname for a pair of Queens. Also known as Ladies or the Hilton Sisters.

Snowmen Holding pocket 8s.

The Doyle Brunson Named after the infamous legend of poker as 10 2 was the hand he won the World Series of Poker with ... twice!

The Four Horsemen When four of a kind (quads) are made from Kings.

The Gay Waiter Queen 3 is known as the 'Gay Waiter' – A Queen with a tres (which is what a 3 is referred to in the US – rhymes with tray).

Three Wise Men A set of Kings.

Transvestite It is an Ace 4 in the hole. When you first turn over the cards it looks like two Aces, but on closer inspection all is not what it seems!

Walking Sticks Pocket 7s. Also known as hockey sticks.

Glossary of terms

Aces up	To be holding two pairs, one of which is Aces.
Action	The betting activity.
All-in	To bet all the money you have on the table.
Ante	A compulsory small bet all players make before a hand is dealt.
Back door	To make a hand you were not originally planning.
Bad beat	To have a better hand defeated by a weaker hand.
Bankroll	Current total gambling funds available.
Belly buster	An inside straight draw also known as a Gutshot.
Bet	To put money/chips into a pot.
Bet for value	Betting a hand that is expected to win more than it loses.
Big Blind	An early compulsory bet, usually double the Small Blind.
Blank	A card that does not help any player's hand.
Blind	A compulsory bet to open the betting.
Bluff	A bet or raise made with a poor or no hand to fool the competition into folding.
Board	The face-up community cards on the table.
Broadway	An Ace-high straight.
Burn	To discard the top card of the deck prior to dealing.
Button	A plastic token placed in front of the player sitting in the nominal dealer's position. If a house dealer is used, the button rotates clockwise around the table so that each player has the opportunity to be the last to act.
Buy-in	The amount of money needed to enter a game.
Call	To place the minimum amount of money/chips into a pot to continue playing.
Caller	The person who makes a call bet.
Calling station	A weak player that often checks or calls most bets.
Calling the clock	To warn a player that he is under a clock (time limit) if he has taken excessive time in acting – usually 30–60 seconds.
Cards speak	At showdown, the final hand values are determined by the face-up cards and not what a player declares.
Case card	The fourth and thus final card of a particular rank to appear on the board.
Change gears	Changing your style of play to suit the game.

Chase	To continue in a hand despite poor odds in hope of getting lucky.
Check	To make no bet when it is legal to do so and thus pass on the action to the next player.
Check raise	To check initially and then raise a bet made later on in the same betting round.
Chip	A round plastic/clay token used in place of cash at the poker table.
Community cards	Cards that are dealt face up in the middle of the table and available for every player to use in making a hand.
Cut the deck	To divide the cards into two fairly even stacks.
Dark bet	To bet without looking at your hand (in the dark).
Dead hand	A misdealt hand that has too many, too few, or exposed cards.
Deuce	A 2.
Double belly buster	A two-way inside straight; for example, 6 8 9 10 J. Also called a double gutshot.
Drawing dead	Drawing to a hand that cannot possibly win no matter which cards fall.
Draw out	To catch a card that changes your hand from a losing to a winning hand.
Early position	Being one of the first players to act in a round of betting.
Face card	Royalty – Jack, Queen or King.
Fish	Someone who is a novice or a poor card player.
Flat-call	To just call the minimum amount of a bet.
Flop	The first three community cards dealt simultaneously and face up.
Flush	A hand consisting of five cards all of the same suit.
Fold	To not call a bet and thus drop out of the hand.
Forced bet	The required bet to start the action – also called a blind.
Fourth Street	The fourth card dealt on the board – also known as the turn.
Free card	The card dealt after all players have checked in a round of betting.
Free-roll	A tournament where there is no buy in fee – usually in online poker.
Freeze-out	A tournament where you do not have the option to re-buy or add-on chips.
Full house	A hand consisting of three-of-a-kind and a pair.
Gutshot	A draw to an inside straight, as in 8 9 J Q.
Heads-up	Playing a single opponent – head-to-head.
Hole cards	The face-down cards dealt to each player.
Hook	A Jack.
House cut	A term for profits taken by the casino for hosting the game.
Implied odds	Money in the pot and money not yet, but expected to be in the pot.
Inside straight	Holding four cards to a straight, with only one rank that will complete the hand, 10 J Q A.

Kicker	The highest side card that is not part of the basic final hand.
Late position	To be seated towards the end of a particular betting round and the positions furthest from the button.
Limp in	To enter a pot as cheaply as possible if there is no or only a minimal raise.
Loose	Playing more hands than most of the other players and making rash calls.
Main pot	The main pot is the one in which all active players participate.
Middle position	To be seated approximately halfway around the table from the button position.
Misdeal	A hand dealt incorrectly that must be redealt.
Muck	A collection of face-down cards near the dealer composed of discards and burn cards.
No-limit poker	A game where there is no maximum bet and a player can wager all the chips in front of her.
Nut flush	The highest possible flush.
Nuts	An unbeatable hand, or the best possible hand at any given point.
Off-suit	Not of the same suit.
On tilt	Playing worse than usual because a player has become emotionally upset.
Open-ended straight	Four cards to a straight in sequence (10 J Q K) with outs at either end.
Outs	The cards that will improve your hand.
Over-pair	A pair in the hole that is larger than any community card on the board.
Pair	Two cards of the same rank.
Pay-off	Calling a bet with little or no expectation of winning and calling to see what the opponent is holding.
Pocket	An individual's starting hole cards.
Position	Player's location in the betting sequence, relative to the players still in the hand.
Pot	The total amount of money bet so far in a hand.
Premium hands	The best possible starting hands.
Quads	Four of a kind.
Rags	Cards that are small to medium, not suited and not in sequence.
Rainbow flop	No matching suits on the board.
Raise	To wager more than the minimum required to call and thus forcing other players to put more money in as well.
Raiser	The player who raises.
Rake	A small percentage of money taken from each pot and given to the house in return for hosting the game.
Read	To assess an opponent's hand by observing his behaviour.

Represent	Implying, by betting, that one has a particular hand.
Re-raise	To raise after an opponent has raised.
Ring game	A standard cash game where players can come and go at will.
River	The last community card dealt in a hand.
Royal flush	An Ace-high straight flush, the best possible hand in regular poker.
Runner-runner	A hand made using both of the last two cards dealt.
Semi-bluff	To bluff with a fairly strong hand that should win if it hits.
Set	Also known as trips, a pair in your hand with a matching rank (or two) on the board.
Short-stacked	Being down to only a small amount of money/chips.
Showdown	The stage at the end of the hand where all active players reveal their cards and the pot is awarded.
Side pot	When an active player runs out of money/chips during the course of a hand, the remaining players participate in a second or side pot for the rest of the hand. Numerous side pots are possible if several players run out of money at different points in a hand.
Slow-play	To play a strong hand weakly/slowly in hopes of trapping at a later stage.
Small Blind	The first player after the button is the Small Blind and posts a compulsory bet/ante, usually one-half the amount of the Big Blind.
Split pot	A pot that is split equally between two or more players.
Stack	The amount of money (the stack of chips) a player has on the table.
Stake	The amount of a player's buy-in, or the amount of money they're willing to play with in a game.
Steal	To win the pot by bluffing.
String bet	An illegal means of raising where a player puts chips into the pot and, after gaining a reaction from another player, adds more chips to the original bet.
Stud	A variety of poker in which some of each players' cards are exposed.
Suited	Two or more cards of the same suit.
Table stakes	A standard rule where players can only bet the money/chips they have on the table.
Tell	A personal mannerism that reveals the quality of one's hand to opponents.
Three of a kind	Three cards, all of the same rank.
Trips	Three of a kind, as in 'Trip Kings'.
Turn	The fourth community card dealt also known as Fourth Street.
Under the gun	The position that has to act first in a round of betting.
Value bet	A small bet to get calls and thereby increase the pot.
Wheel	An A 2 3 4 5. The best possible low hand. Also called a Bicycle.

Acknowledgements

Executive editor
Trevor Davies

Editor
Emma Pattison

Executive art editor
Penny Stock

Designer
Barbara Zuniga

Illustrator
Sean Sims

Senior production controller
Martin Croshaw